No Time For
DYING

No Time For
DYING

BY EDDIE HARRISON
AND
ALFRED V. J. PRATHER

PRENTICE-HALL, INC.
Englewood Cliffs, New Jersey

No Time for Dying by Eddie Harrison and Alfred V. J. Prather

Copyright © 1973 by Eddie Harrison and Alfred V. J. Prather

Printed in the United States of America

Prentice-Hall International, Inc., London
Prentice-Hall of Australia, Pty. Ltd., North Sydney
Prentice-Hall of Canada, Ltd., Toronto
Prentice-Hall of India Private Ltd., New Delhi
Prentice-Hall of Japan, Inc., Tokyo

Library of Congress Cataloging in Publication Data

Harrison, Eddie, 1942–
No time for dying.

1. Prisoners—United States—Personal narratives.
I. Prather, Alfred V. J., 1926–   II. Title.
HV9468.H25   364.1′523′0924 [B]   72-8375
ISBN 0-13-622894-1

To those we love

EDDIE and AL

INTRODUCTION

As a former Attorney General of the Commonwealth of Massachusetts I have retained a deep and continuing interest in the method by which those men and women who serve time in our penal system are transformed from burdens on society to contributing members of the community to which one day they will return.

The method we have used and continue to use to accomplish this end has conclusively proven to be a gross failure. The vast majority of our prisons and institutions offer not even the hope of rehabilitation. The despair, fear, frustration, and degradation which are endemic to these institutions all too often culminate in the loss of precious life—or in a living death.

Why must it take an Attica before society realizes it has an obligation to the men, women, and children it has "put away," but who will return? Why must people committed to our correctional institutions fight desperately and alone to maintain their own core of human decency, when one of the purposes of sending people to institutions is to teach them to be "decent" human beings? Why have we not created within this great country a system which responds to the needs of all Americans?

These questions are unanswered and will go unanswered as long as we, as a society, turn our backs on those who need and deserve our attention. The poor and uneducated and disadvantaged of America make up the bulk of our prison population. They become criminals because there is little opportunity or incentive for any other kind of achievement.

Alternatives can be found to our present deplorable system. We need only turn our attention to search for them and to apply them.

In seeking methods to address these problems, we must

be willing to experiment, and encourage those who would lead in these experiments. We must understand that *no* institution can succeed, or even survive, without the involvement and participation of the community it serves, but that all of us—corrections officers, inmates, and citizens—can find the answers together. The salvation of many human lives is at stake, and the betterment of society as well.

No Time For Dying answers many questions. But it poses many more. It is one man's story, but it is typical of thousands of nameless, faceless young men in this country who are dehumanized by our criminal justice system.

It is the story of one man who survived the system. But there are thousands of Eddie Harrisons in our institutions today who are fighting to save their humanity. Some will succeed, and some will fail.

The point of this book is that all of them deserve more of a chance to help themselves.

No Time For Dying very carefully reveals the many pitfalls, obstacles, and injustices that afflict not only Black Americans, but the poor and other minority group members who are not afforded equal protection under the law. This is the story of two men—a prisoner and his lawyer—who possessed exceptional faith and conviction.

They found each other and combined their efforts in a quest for justice.

The trials of Eddie Harrison serve as an indictment of our criminal justice system. One court consistently reversed another through four separate trials. Finally the President of the United States was called upon to exercise his executive powers.

This is where I became involved in Eddie Harrison's case, where I, too, was persuaded of the justice of his cause. And where, together, we won an unprecedented presidential commutation.

Eddie Harrison and Al Prather refused to give up, and

their efforts were successful. But such effort should not be required to secure simple justice. Justice is for all men; let us make it so.

Edward W. Brooke
United States Senate

CONTENTS

No Time For
DYING

1

Pawning the Shotgun

(Eddie)

"As your attorney, I advise you to plead guilty to second-degree murder. That's the only thing that can save you." These words, spoken by Mr. Perry W. Howard, attorney-at-law, were in the beginning of a nightmare which was to last for nearly nine years.

The chain of events leading to those words began on March 7, 1960, in the R. C. Restaurant at North Capitol and P Streets, NW, in Washington, D.C. I was seated at the lunch counter, having coffee with some of my friends. Most of the rap was about police brutality, no jobs, girls, clothes, cars, the latest records and dances—idle conversation with little or no significance. I had recently dropped out of high school to find work and help support my family. I had gone to the coffee shop to find out if there were any jobs open where the other fellows worked.

Around 10:00 P.M. Orson White showed up and sat down next to me. Orson and I had been friends for years and had often looked for jobs together. He had heard that there were jobs at a construction site in Maryland, and we decided that we would check it out the following morning.

We left to find Jimmy Evans, a friend of mine, who would loan me one of his cars. We found Jimmy on Seventh Street with some other dudes. Of particular interest was Joseph "Ray" Sampson. I told Jimmy of my plans and he said I could use his Buick. Sampson asked if he could go with us to the Maryland construction company. I didn't have a driver's license and Sampson appeared to be the answer to our other problem—someone to drive the car. Jimmy thought I had a license and I did nothing to change that impression. Jimmy and I went to his home to pick up the Buick. I drove it back to Seventh Street and picked up Orson White and Ray Sampson. I drove them home around midnight and then went to my home.

My grandmother was still up, and we talked about the possibilities of my getting a job. She was very optimistic and impressed with my intentions. The car was low on gas and I was thinking of this when I went to bed. Before dropping off to sleep I had a reassuring thought. "I can pawn my shotgun to Cider Brown in the morning and have enough money to buy gas and lunch while I'm in Maryland."

After breakfast on the morning of March 8 I put my shotgun in the trunk of the car and went to George's house. George Brown, alias "Cider George," was the neighborhood loan shark. He would loan money on anything if he thought he could resell it for a profit. The morning was very quiet and still. A faint chill in the air was refreshing. Arriving at George's house, I parked and went to his door. I left the gun in the car because it was early and I really didn't think that he would be home, but since I was already in the neighborhood I gave it a try. I knocked several times but there was no answer. Finally I gave up and decided to pick the other fellows up first and return later.

I remembered from the night before that Sampson also

lived on Fourth Street, but I couldn't remember the house he had gone into so I went to get Orson first because he knew where Sampson lived. Orson was just finishing breakfast, and he came out almost immediately. I asked him if he had any money for gas. He said he wanted to save his for lunch. We then proceeded to Sampson's house.

When Sampson came out, I got out of the driver's seat and told him to wait a minute. I went to the trunk of the car and got the shotgun, and then opened the back door of the car and threw the gun on the floor. I got into the back of the car and told Sampson to drive us to the 1500 block of Fourth Street before going to Maryland.

This time I saw George's car parked in front of his house. I told Sampson to park and said I would be right back. Sampson parked on the corner of Fourth and R Streets and I picked up the gun and got out of the car. I went to George's house alone because I didn't think that he knew Sampson or White and figured he would be reluctant to do business in their presence. As I approached George's house, the outer door was open. I stepped into the vestibule and knocked on the door. There was no answer. After a few moments I knocked again and heard George answer, "Just a minute." I had the shotgun in my hand, holding it very loosely. Just then the thought occurred to me that perhaps the gun was loaded and that I'd better check to make sure it was not!

At this point, I also remembered that the gun couldn't possibly be loaded because I had just gotten it back from George about a week before and I had not touched it since that time. I was going to check it anyway to be sure, but my thoughts were interrupted by George pulling back the shade of the door to see who was there. After seeing that it was me, he asked, "You got something for me?" I replied, "Yes, I have a gun!"

"Let me see it. Come on in."

I stepped back a little to raise the shotgun from my side

to present it to him for inspection, just as he started to open the door. The door was opening and the gun was waist high. I was holding the gun in the middle as I stepped forward.

At that moment, George looked beyond me and seemed startled for a brief second. Then the door was slammed in my face. As a reflex motion, I jerked the gun up to prevent it from breaking the glass as the door was closing. The gun hit the glass window and went off. I had never heard a sound as loud as this. It sounded like a tremendous explosion. I was knocked against the opposite wall of the vestibule. A thousand thoughts flashed into my mind.

"You've broken the glass!"
"Run!"
"You'll have to pay for it!"
"You'll get in trouble!"
"Who loaded the gun?"
"Police!"
"Hurt!"
"Pain!"
"Run!"
"George will be mad!"
"He won't loan you the money now!"
"Police!"
"Beating!"
"Run!"
"Run!"
"Run!"

My mind raced on and on in this split second. I got up off the floor and ran. To my great surprise, Orson was standing in the doorway and I almost knocked him down. Time had no meaning. It seemed as though I had been in the vestibule for hours, but actually it was only for a few minutes. Orson had a shocked expression on his face when I ran into him, an expression of horror, an unbelieving stare. I was unaware that I was still holding the gun in my hand as I ran out of the doorway. Orson ran behind me. He was yelling to me to stop but I kept on running. Sampson was in the car waiting, but I paid no attention to him either. I ran past the car and continued to run as fast as my legs would carry me.

I didn't see Orson stop and get in the car. My mind pushed me on; "RUN, RUN, RUN." Sampson drove the car ahead of me and stopped.

Seeing them brought me back to reality. I jumped into the car. Sampson and White were yelling at me. "What happened? What happened, man?"

I wanted to answer, to explain that I didn't mean to break the window, but I couldn't answer! I didn't know what had happened. I was confused. How could the gun go off? Was George hurt? Maybe dead? By now we were approaching the 1200 block of Fourth Street, where I lived, and I told Sampson to stop the car. I got out and ran into the house. My grandmother had gone out, so I went into the backyard and put the gun in the trash can.

After that, I didn't know what to do or where to go. I considered calling the police but ruled that out because of other dealings I'd had with them. Finally I decided to change clothes and go back to George's house to find out exactly what had happened. I went back to the car and told Sampson and White to meet me at a friend's house in a little while. I walked around for an hour or so and then went back to George's house.

There was a large crowd of people in front of the house, and several police officers. Some police were inside the house and others were going in through the front window. I mingled with the crowd and worked my way to the foot of the steps. I heard someone say that George had been shot and was hurt very badly. A policeman was moving through the crowd asking questions and taking people's names. I got scared, so I moved away from the crowd and left. I walked the streets for hours trying to figure out what to do. I was drastically afraid to go to the police because I didn't trust them: they were to be feared; they would not believe me. They would beat the hell out of me and then put me in jail. No! I could not go to the police. Just wait and see what happens.

That evening I went uptown—Fourteenth and U Streets in the heart of the red-light district. Everyone was talking about what had occurred, but they didn't seem to understand that it was an accident. Everywhere I went, the conversation was centered around "the murder of Cider George." I was upset to discover that George was dead, and more confused than ever as to what I should do. I went home and tried to figure out a course of action. I was torn between a desire to run and hide, and a reluctant inclination to turn myself over to the authorities.

My family sensed my obviously disturbed frame of mind and asked me if anything was wrong. Said I was just tired from the long ride to Maryland looking for a job. I went to bed early but sleep would not come. I was very restless and afraid that if I closed my eyes, the police would find me and take me to jail.

The following morning I went back into the streets and bought a newspaper. The headlines jumped out at me:

"GAMBLER MURDERED"
"POLICE LOOKING FOR KILLERS"
"GANGLAND-TYPE SLAYING"
"KILLERS VANISH"

I was determined never to claim knowledge of the incident because they would surely put me in jail for the rest of my life. Perhaps even kill me!

On the morning of March 10 I went to Stanley Stevenson's house, where I was supposed to have met Sampson and White two days earlier.

Stanley was taking a bath, so I went into the living room. Sampson and White were there, along with a girl who I later learned was Wilma Jean Russell, a girl friend of Stanley. The three of us chatted for a while concerning the rumors and newspaper stories of the past few days.

Stanley finished his bath and came into the living room with a towel around his middle. He walked to the window and looked out. Suddenly he yelled, "Man, there are cops all over the place!" I ran to the back door and there were policemen there too. I came back and told them, and we all stayed in the living room and closed the door.

There was a loud knock at the front door, but no one moved. The quietness in the room was deafening. Again the loud knock, but still no answer. The door was crashed in, the lock broken. Loud footsteps on the stairway and then a knock on the living room door. Still no answer from within. The door was torn from its hinges. The police streamed into the room, with angry faces and their guns drawn.

Everyone was ordered to raise his hands and lean against the wall to be searched. Stanley demanded an explanation and a warrant for this entry. He was knocked to the floor in response. The policemen searched the house without hesitating, as though they knew exactly what they were looking for and where to look. The clothing was pulled from the closet and thrown to the floor in a pile. The beds were taken apart and searched, the tables, chairs, ceiling lights.

Stanley, lying on the floor, was pulled to his feet and told to put on certain articles of clothing that the policemen had chosen from the pile on the floor. No questions were asked. The girl was taken into another room and we were escorted from the house and to a patrol wagon. En route to the station, everyone agreed not to acknowledge anything concerning the incident. We knew what to expect when we arrived at the station, but still we agreed not to talk.

We were taken to the Homicide Squad of the Metropolitan Police Department for questioning. Each of us was taken into a different room and the questioning began. I was in a chair facing one of the arresting detectives, who was sitting at a desk. Another detective was pacing the floor, chewing gum and clenching his fists. He walked behind me and I listened very intently for the sound of his footsteps. I felt a crushing blow to the back of my neck which knocked me to the floor. The pain was unbearable but I didn't cry out. I lay there waiting for the kick which was sure to follow.

He told me to get up and to be careful or I would "fall" out of the chair again. I was told to put my hat on; they wanted to see if I fit the description of a rape suspect they were looking for. I put the hat on and sat there. The detective walked behind me and I braced myself for the blow. He knocked my hat to the floor in front of me and told me to pick it up. I bent over to pick up the hat and felt a sharp pain in my chest which forced me back, knocking the wind from my lungs. I lay on the floor gasping for breath and I was kicked again in the lower part of my body—on my legs, thighs, and stomach.

The detective seated at the desk told the other one to stop and leave the room. I got a look at his face as I got up off of the floor. He was wearing an amused grin, showing some type of physical pleasure at inflicting this pain upon me. I stored an image of his face away in my subconscious mind for the day when I could get my revenge for the humiliation and pain that I had suffered.

The other detective began questioning me. "Where were you on the morning of March 8?" I refused to answer.

He told me a woman had been beaten and raped and that I was only there for questioning concerning the rape. I told him that I didn't know anything about anyone being raped.

His eyes gleamed as I answered him. He told me if the statement were true, I had nothing to worry about. I was beginning to feel more at ease, so I relaxed a little. I was asked to take a lie detector test concerning the rape. I then realized that the rape incident was fabricated for the purpose of getting me on the lie detector.

With this thought in mind, I replied that I would be glad to take a lie detector test but not until I had an opportunity to calm my nerves. He made a phone call and talked for several minutes, after which he told me that the juvenile authorities were on the way and that I was to be turned over to them. I could hear sounds coming from another room. Someone was being beaten very badly. I began to wonder why the questioning had stopped and then realized because I was seventeen the police didn't have authority over me and probably were afraid to turn me over to the juvenile authorities with evidence of police brutality. I wasn't scarred or cut, but I was certainly in pain.

I was turned over to the juvenile authorities and taken to the Receiving Home for Boys, where I was detained until the next morning. Then I was taken back to police headquarters and again questioned. I still refused to answer any questions concerning the incident. I wanted to rid myself of the knowledge that I possessed, but I couldn't bring myself to confide in the police. How could a person possibly trust a police officer?

I was released from custody around noontime. My chest felt as though there was a foreign object embedded there, and with each breath I felt a terrific amount of pain. I went home and bathed in very hot water to soothe the aches and pains. My grandmother asked me where I had spent the night and I lied. I told her that I had slept at my aunt's house. Luckily my mother was at work, or I would not have gotten away with it so easily. I ate a late breakfast and went to my room to lie down. I was very tired and I felt as though I could sleep forever, but that was not the case. I couldn't sleep. For all my weariness, I could not sleep! I couldn't shut my mind to the reality of the situation that I was in, nor could I find relief from the burdening knowledge that I possessed. I desperately wanted someone to confide in. Orson and Sampson didn't even know what actually happened, and oddly enough, neither did I!

I lay there reconstructing in my mind the events of the morning of March 8. I thought of the gun, and I jumped out of bed and went to the window. The trash can had been emptied; I sighed in relief. I went back to bed and my thoughts went back to a few weeks before. George had been holding the gun for about three weeks. Stanley Stevenson told me that George wanted me to come and get it back or he was going to sell it. I distinctly remember having opened the gun when I gave it to George and checking to see that it was not loaded. He gave me ten dollars and I was to pay him twelve dollars to get it back. After one week the interest would be one dollar per day.

I went to get the gun back about two weeks before the incident occurred, but I did not check it when he gave it to me. The only way the gun could have been loaded was if George had loaded it himself for some purpose! Why would he load the gun and give it back to me loaded?

I thought of many apparent reasons why he would load the gun. Then I suddenly realized why he slammed the door in my face. I sat up in bed and screamed, "NO!" When I was stepping through the door to enter his house, Orson had come up the steps, and at that point George's eyes looked beyond me and he had a frightened expression on his face. His reason for loading the gun must have been to use it for protection against being robbed. He must have slammed the door in my face because he didn't recognize Orson White and thought this was an attempted robbery!

Everything tied in!

According to the newspaper, he had approximately $2,000 on his person. I was standing there with a gun. Orson was coming in the door. George was the only one who could have misunderstood the circumstances, and his reaction to what appeared to be a dangerous situation was to slam the door.

I then realized that I was in very serious trouble. The questions began to flash through my mind again.

Why did Orson come into the vestibule?

Why did the police come to Stanley's?

Would anyone believe me?

Did they tell the police anything?

Did the police let them go?

I got out of bed, put my clothes on, and went out into the street. I called Orson's home and found out that he was not there and had not been there all night. I didn't know Sampson's phone number so I went back to Stanley's house. No one was home, which made me conclude that they were still in police custody.

I wandered the streets, worrying whether or not the police were just around the corner getting ready to grab me. They always come when you least expect them.

I went to the R. C. Restaurant and ordered coffee. The place was busy and everyone was talking about Cider George. There was speculation concerning his death. Some believed it was because he had not paid off a "numbers hit"; others thought he was set up by the syndicate for not turning in his receipts. Still others thought it was a robbery attempt. I wanted to venture that it was probably some sort of accident, but I dared not open my mouth. Of one thing I was certain: I would never tell the police or anyone else about my involvement in the death of Cider George.

The newspapers carried an article that day, and the police were quoted as saying they were "very close to making an arrest" in the Cider George slaying. I spent the next few days wondering how long it would take them to catch up with me.

The evening of March 16 found me again in the R. C. Restaurant. My friend Eugene Valentine came in, and we started talking about things in general. Eventually the conversation worked itself around to Cider George. Eugene asked me if they had caught the dudes who shot Cider. In response I stated point-blank: "I killed him!"

I was expecting to feel a sense of relief. But instead, I felt a sense of pride! Somehow I wanted to be connected with the notoriety of being involved in such a newsworthy case. To hear people whisper my name, to be world-known, to be connected with the syndicate and big league "hooddom." To be acclaimed as the man who killed Cider George. I felt elated, a big-time gangster who would be admired by the rest of the hustlers. I completely disregarded the facts and invented circumstances to further the image of my being a big-time hood. I told Eugene that it looked as if he were going for his gun and I shot him! Little did I know or care that this lie, this admission prompted by false pride, would be one of the most important elements in keeping me in prison all those years.

Our conversation was interrupted at this point because some other people had entered the restaurant. I was watching Eugene for his reactions, and I could plainly see that he was impressed and to some degree envious!

On the morning of March 18, my eighteenth birthday, I called Eugene and told him that I was going to borrow a car and that I wanted to use his identification and driver's permit. I got the car from Jimmy Evans and drove to Eugene's house. We exchanged wallets. We both fit the same general description and would easily pass a "spot check" if it occurred. I told him my plans were to pick up a girl in Southeast and one for him in Southwest. Then we would go uptown to a nightclub and have a little private birthday party.

Around 9:30 P.M., coming back into Northwest via the Sousa Bridge, I was leaning a little heavy on the accelerator when I noticed a motorcycle policeman approaching me. When we passed each other I was doing at least seventy miles an hour. He immediately turned around and came after me, siren screaming.

I stopped, hoping I would only receive a ticket for speeding. I got out of the car before he reached me. I tried to be cheerful and make his job as easy as possible. I waited for him to speak so that I could determine what type of cop he was.

Finally he said, "Where's the fire, buddy?" and reached for his "write-up pad."

I replied, "I guess you're right, I'm not going to argue that I wasn't speeding because I was. You see, it's my birthday and I'm trying to get home before the party starts. I deserve the ticket, but it's a birthday gift that I really didn't expect!"

He found the remark humorous but he continued to write the ticket. He wrote the tag number down and then it occurred to me that the car didn't have an inspection sticker on it! The officer sensed my change of mood and asked for my driver's license. Then he asked for the registration and I got it out of the glove compartment for him. He still had not noticed that the sticker was missing, and I was trying to keep him away from that side of the car. He asked me my name and I told him, "Benjamin Eugene Valentine." I gave him the address also, and he handed me a ticket.

His attention went to the other occupants in the car, and he walked around to the passenger side and looked inside the car. He asked Eugene his name and Eugene said, "My name is Eddie Harrison."

The officer seemed startled to hear the name. He stepped back for a second and repeated the question.

"What is your name?"

"Eddie M. Harrison," came the reply. He then noticed that the car did not have an inspection sticker. He told me to get into the car and follow him to the station.

I almost ran, but decided to play it through to the end.

En route to the police station the girl asked me what was wrong and I told her that we had to go to the station to pay for a speeding ticket and that it would only take a few minutes.

At the police station, we were taken into a large room and the motorcycle cop went into an adjoining room and spoke to a detective. The detective didn't seem particularly interested until he heard the name Eddie Harrison. Suddenly he turned to look at Eugene with an inquisitive stare. The two of them then came over and asked our names again. I repeated that I was Eugene Valentine and Eugene stated that he was Eddie Harrison. The detective left the room and made a phone call. I took out a package of ciga-rettes and was offered a match by the motorcycle cop. After lighting my cigarette, he told me to keep the book of matches and I put them in my pocket.

I asked him if we were under arrest and he said, "Not really, you just have to wait until the tickets are made out." We sat there for about forty-five minutes, until two other detectives came in, along with a matron from the Woman's Division. The girl was taken out of the room and searched. The detective then ordered Eugene and me to put all of our personal effects on the table. One of the detectives pulled a small brown envelope from his pocket. He showed the contents to the motorcycle cop, who looked up quickly with a hard, unblinking stare. He then walked over to me and said, "Give me my damn matches back!"

I held out the matches and he snatched them from my hand angrily and told me to stand up. He turned to the detective and said, "Let's search this bastard!"

The sudden change in his attitude told me that he had found out I was Eddie Harrison and that I could abandon all hope of keeping up the masquerade. Eugene was taken from the room and I was left alone with the two detectives and the motorcycle cop.

I knew then that they were getting ready for the "rough

stuff." With this thought barely through my conscious mind, I was slammed against the wall by one of the detectives.

It's a little game they play before questioning a suspect. It's called "Good Guy, Bad Guy." One of them will slap you around for a while and then the other one will make him stop. "Bad Guy" leaves the room while "Good Guy" questions you. If you don't answer the questions, "Bad Guy" comes back.

After my session with "Bad Guy," "Good Guy" asked me my name.

I replied, "My name is Benjamin Eugene Valentine."

Just then, "Bad Guy" stepped forward and held out a mug shot of me.

"Who in the hell is this then, Mr. Benjamin Eugene Valentine?"

The sight of my picture removed all doubts of what was going to happen. I refused to reply.

"You're eighteen now, huh?"

Still no reply. I then realized that I had not been wrong. The net had been thrown and now it was being drawn tight. I had not responded to "Good Guy, Bad Guy," so I waited for the second act to begin. It didn't take very long.

"We know who you are, Eddie, so let's stop pretending."

"Good Guy" was talking in a low, calm voice just dripping with kindness and compassion.

"We just want to question you about a housebreaking, that's all."

Act Two had begun. A fictitious crime for the purpose of getting me to agree to a lie detector test. I had expected an offense more serious than housebreaking, though.

He continued: "Look, son, my partner thinks he can go around beating information out of people, but I won't let him beat you any more if you tell me all about it."

The question popped into my mind: What "it" is he talking about? Now the game changes to psychology.

"I know you didn't mean it, Eddie, so come on and let me help you. That's what I get paid for. To help people in trouble."

"Bad Guy" was nervously pacing the floor with his arms folded behind his back. He seemed to be waiting for "Good Guy" to give up and turn me over to him again.

Still no response from me.

As if on signal, "Good Guy" shrugged his shoulders and "Bad Guy" was right on the job.

"All right, goddamn it, where in the hell is that shotgun?"

I was startled at the point-blank question. I was snatched up from the chair by the lapels of my coat and again thrown against the wall. . . .

Nineteen-sixty was a very good year for police brutality. A man could walk down the street, get arrested on suspicion of anything imaginable, taken to a police station, get beaten almost to death, and end up charged with assault on a police officer. The streets of Washington, D.C., definitely were not safe, and not all of the danger came from the criminal element that exists there.

". . . Can't talk, huh?"

"Weren't you arrested in connection with the Cider Brown murder?"

I couldn't have answered if I wanted to. The question came as a shock and I was completely knocked off guard. I was more determined than ever not to say anything about the incident, regardless of how much I would have to suffer. "Bad Guy," big, ugly, and black, told the motorcycle cop to book me and to "clear the books."

I was charged with housebreaking, driving without a license, speeding, driving a prohibited vehicle, drunk, and disorderly. After being booked, I was taken to Number 10 Police Station and again beaten. The officers at No. 10 were professionals at inflicting pain—but I still refused to answer any questions. My attitude and stubbornness seemed to be fuel for their anger. I was in pain and mentally exhausted. There were moments when I would have agreed to almost anything in order to stop being beaten.

I had been in custody for approximately ten hours but it seemed like weeks.

I was taken to the Court of General Sessions and an attorney was appointed to represent me on the traffic offenses. After a brief interview with him outside of the courtroom, in which he advised me to plead guilty to all counts and place myself at the mercy of the court, I was taken before a judge. He sentenced me to sixty days in jail for the traffic charges, and I was held on the housebreaking charge with a $5,000 bond.

I had forgotten all about the housebreaking charge, but apparently the police had not! The session before the Honorable Judge lasted for about five minutes, and then I was rushed to the lock-up cells in the rear of the courtroom to wait to be taken to jail. After a brief time I was transferred to the central cell block unit in the basement of the court building. There, I stood at the entrance to a large cage and waited for the guard to open the door. There were approximately fifty men waiting there to go to jail. They were a foul bunch—mostly drunks sleeping on the floor or lying on the iron cots suspended from the wall by chains. There were no sheets or mattresses on the cots; they were just iron slabs. The men didn't seem to notice the inconvenience of not having sheets or pillows; all of the cots were occupied, some by two or more people. The stench was immediately noticeable, a strong acid-like smell that made me not want to breathe—unwashed bodies, urine that never reached the urinal, stale whiskey on unwashed mouths. Strangely, I was glad to be here, away from the pounding fists, the kicking feet, and the pain and agony that go with being questioned by the cops.

The guard opened the door and I was shoved inside, stumbling over groaning bodies that never moved. There

was no space to sit down, not even on the floor. I thought
I would vomit from the rotten smell of the people. I moved
into a corner and leaned against the wall. It was around
10:00 A.M. and I thought that I would soon be moved to the
jail, where I could rest. Nothing seemed important anymore. All I wanted to do was rest, to lie on clean white
sheets and sleep, to relax my aching body. I had never been
so tired in my life.

I stayed in this cage for approximately eight hours.
Around five o'clock I heard the sound of a bus driving up
to the door. Someone yelled, "Transport Bus, D.C. Jail."

There was a sound of heavy keys and a loud voice: "What
took you so damn long? Let's get these drunks out of
here!"

Two U.S. marshals came around to the front of the cage,
each carrying a large ring of handcuffs. The guard opened
the front of the cage and banged the keys against the bars,
yelling:

"All right, let's go. Get up, let's go, damn it. Get your
ass up off that bunk!"

The marshals called off a list of names one at a time and
the men began to shuffle forward. When my name was
called, I stepped forward and was handcuffed to an old
man, obviously drunk and visibly dirty and ragged. I hurried forward, wishing not to touch him but pulling the old
man along.

The bus was waiting, silently sitting there, drinking up
the steady flow of humanity that came out of the lock-up.
The bus was large, gray in color, and carried with it the
unmistakable stench of unwashed bodies. Inside the bus I
discovered that it was hardly a bus at all, but rather a cage
on wheels.

It filled up beyond maximum capacity; men were jammed
in the aisles. The odor was becoming more unbearable by
the second. I tried to open the window but discovered that
it wasn't meant to be opened. At the same time I discovered

that there was no cord to pull if you wanted to get off.

I started to smile. Why should there be a cord?

We sat there for approximately thirty minutes and the other marshal came out and boarded the bus. After the last man was pushed into the cage, the marshal locked the gate and turned on a fan. I expected the fan to eliminate the horrible smell, but it only served to circulate the foul air. The bus began to move in a circular motion and it seemed odd until I realized that we were parked on a turntable. We were pointed toward a large steel door, and at the push of a button it began to fold back.

The men swayed with the motion of the bus as we went up Massachusetts Avenue and around the circle in front of Union Station. Ten minutes' drive and we were approaching the District of Columbia Jail. I had read newspaper articles concerning the District Jail. It was formally called the "Washington Jail and Asylum." It's a large, red stone building surrounded by double barbed-wire fences. As we approached the jail in the dark, the lights were turned on, flooding the building and the immediate grounds with a bright, watchful glare. The bus turned into the driveway and stopped in front of the huge tower. The driver opened his window and spoke into a speaker located on the side of the tower:

"U.S. Marshal with forty-nine prisoners from General Sessions Court."

We sat there while the driver gave his pistol to the other marshal, who deposited it, along with his own, in a dumbwaiter at the foot of the tower. The marshal reboarded the bus, and the huge iron gate slid back smoothly to let us enter. We drove through, only to be confronted by a second gate, which opened as soon as the first one clanged shut.

We drove to the side of the building and the bus seemed to come alive at this point. The men started to push forward, seemingly anxious to get into the jail. I could see prisoners looking out of the windows with blank, disinterested expressions on their faces.

The marshal went up to a steel door and pushed a button on the wall; a few seconds later the door opened, accompanied by a loud electrical buzz. When the door was completely open, the marshal turned and yelled to the driver:

"All right, let them go!"

The driver opened the cage door and the men streamed out, pulling each other, some stumbling and being dragged out. The old man who was handcuffed to me started to get up and add to the confusion, but I pulled him back into the seat. I had endured the stench of him this far and I could stand it for a few more minutes.

We finally got off and walked up the steps into the jail. We were in the basement, in what is called the "control center"—a series of iron-bar cages, all operated by electric gates; in the center is a glass-enclosed operations center manned by four officers.

There was a loud click, and the gate facing the control center was opened. The marshals were in the process of removing the handcuffs and the officer in the cage was sorting papers and checking names against another sheet. The officer spoke with a loud voice, full of authority:

"Give me your attention. Put out all cigarettes and listen for your name to be called. If you left this jail to go to court this morning, answer 'return' when your name is called and step to the back of the hall; if you did not leave this jail this morning, answer 'new man' when your name is called and step to the back of the hall. There will be no talking.

"Eddie Harrison."

I stepped forward and walked up to the gate. The officer looked at me, obviously waiting for me to say something or do something. I said that I was a new man and he told me to step to the rear of the hall. I stood there for a second, wondering if I should ask him if I could see a doctor. My ribs were beginning to throb with pain and I had a terrible headache. Before I could speak, he yelled again for me to step to the rear of the hall and I moved on.

I stood leaning against the bars for two hours. At last an officer came down the hall in my direction and I focused my attention on him. He was around seven feet tall, very clumsy looking, with a blank expression on his face. He carried a large ring of keys in his hand and bounced them against his leg as he walked. The door clicked as if in warning and swiftly slid open. He called to the officer in the cage. "I've got them."

In a much louder voice he spoke to the crowd of men: "All right, let's move out. Stay close to the wall on the right and go straight back to the iron door."

We moved past him and he began counting us. Like sheep we streamed past the shepherd. As I walked down the hall, I noticed steam pipes overhead dripping water on the cracked concrete floor. The walls were also concrete with large gaping cracks in them. One other thing was immediately noticeable: the smell had changed from horrible to nauseating.

When we reached the other door, a guard stationed there immediately opened the door for us. We entered a large area, also composed of cages. This area was called R and D (Receiving and Discharge). The first cage led into another which opened into a large area containing clothing racks and a search table. We were told to be seated in the first cage and wait for instructions.

After being fingerprinted, photographed, and searched, I was given my jail clothes. The officer in charge of the cell block informed me that I could have one phone call made for me by an official of the jail, and that I would get the answer from the call in a few days. He gave me a pamphlet containing the rules and regulations, and finally, after telling me that I could take all the food I wanted at meals but must eat everything that I took, he assigned me to a cell and gave me two sheets, a towel, and a pillowcase.

I was escorted up two flights of stairs and taken to the third tier. I was told to go down the tier and stand in front of cell 315. Walking down the tier, I could see the occupants of the other cells. They all appeared to have one thing in common: nothing to do.

Most of the men were simply staring at the walls from various positions. Some were sitting on little steel benches protruding from the wall or lying on the beds and staring at the ceiling, while others were pacing the floor like caged animals. As I continued on down the tier, I noticed one other thing—nearly all of the men were young and black. I stood in front of my cell. The guard yelled, "Watch your hands," and began turning a crank at the far end of the tier. The barred steel door of cell 315 slowly opened and I was told to step inside. As I did so, the door began to close —and for a brief moment I had the impulse to run and scream at the top of my voice, "No! No! No!" The door closed with a loud clanking sound and I was overcome by a feeling of being completely, hopelessly trapped. It wasn't just a feeling—it was stark reality!

I stepped up to the bars and leaned against them; they were cold to the touch. I tried to shake them and anger began to swell my chest. Realizing the hopelessness of my attempt, I leaned my head against the cold steel bars and closed my eyes. I stood there for a second and was startled to hear a voice within the cell:

"What are you in for, buddy?" I turned to notice a fellow lying on the bunk bed against the wall. "Ain't no sense in shaking them bars, Jack. They ain't gonna move one bit."

The voice came from the darkness under the top bunk. I could see the glow of a cigarette and could smell something that vaguely resembled tobacco. He got up from the bed, and I could tell from his shadow that he was a huge man. My anger suddenly turned to fear. I wanted out. He turned the light on and faced me. To my surprise and great relief, I knew him!

"Hey, John, what's happening man?"

"Damn, Eddie, I didn't know that was you. What you get popped for, baby?"

"I got a murder beef, man; you know that Cider George thing?"

"Damn, Jack, I been reading about that. I thought somebody set him up because he didn't pay off a numbers hit. You know how that sucker was about paying off them hits? I was going to down him myself because he tried to get out on me once. What happened, man? Run it down to me."

I didn't know whether to tell him the truth or stick with the other story. He didn't wait for an answer—more questions.

"Who's on the beef with you? Who busted you? Come on, man, run it!"

"Look, man, I'll tell you about it tomorrow. I'm tired and sore right now; them rollers beat the hell outa me and all I want to do is lay down!"

"You know, I told that punk on the desk to put a young boy in the cell with me. I thought you was some 'action' when you first came in. Wait till I see that chump in the morning. I should kick his ass for putting a gangster in my cell!"

I felt pride at being called a gangster. I decided that I would live up to the title and stick to the lie.

"What's happening in the streets, man? You know, I been in this joint for two years."

"Ain't nothing happening, man. The rollers are messing with everybody. You can't even walk downtown without getting jammed. There's a panic on and all the junkies are uptight for scagg. Them fools are knocking off drugstores and doctor's offices trying to get down. All the honkeys in Georgetown got the jive uptight, and the hustlers uptown are cutting each others' throats trying to make a dime. You know how it is out in that jungle, man. If you ain't hip to a good hustle, you can't make it."

"You been through this joint before?"

"Naw. I'll hip you to some of them hacks tomorrow, too. You going to chow in the morning?"

"What time is chow?"

"Five thirty."

"Five thirty!"

"Yeah."

"Hell, no!"

"You got a lawyer for that murder beef?"

"Look, man, I ain't charged with it yet. All I got right now is a bunch of traffic charges and a jive meatball housebreaking charge."

"A housebreaking?"

"Yeah, they gave me a housebreaking charge and a five-grand bond to keep me in. You know how they do you when they want to hold you in. I can't make bond for ninety days anyway because of the traffic charges. They tried to kill me at the precinct, man, but all they got outa me was a hard time."

"That's right, Jack, don't tell them suckers nothing. Even if they jam you and put you in the hole."

I didn't know what the "hole" was, but I could tell that it was no place to go!

I jumped up on the bed and pulled my pants, shirt, and shoes off.

"You say you thought I was some action, huh? I think I'll punch that chump in the face myself tomorrow for trying to set me up. What's that sucker's name, anyway?"

"Don't bother him, man, I'll straighten him out tomorrow. Did you file an appeal to the traffic charges?"

Did I file an appeal? I didn't know what he was talking about again but I said "Yeah" anyway. "I'll rap to you in the morning, Jim, I'm tired as hell."

"Okay, Jack, I'll check with you in the morning."

I tried to go to sleep, but sleep wouldn't come. As tired and weary as my body was, my mind wouldn't let it rest.

Again I felt the pain in my side. I thought about asking John if I could see a doctor but decided against it because I was just too damn sore to get up.

I lay there thinking about the events that led to my being in jail, wondering what had happened to Orson and Ray, wondering how my family would react when they found out I was locked up.

Suddenly I heard noises coming from some point behind my cell. It sounded like the inmates were rioting. There was the sound of tin cups being raked against the bars and a chant—hey, hey, hey, hey!

The noise was deafening.

I asked John, "What's going on, man?"

"Nothing. It's time for the shift to change and the guys are just raising hell to cause confusion and keep the hacks from getting off. Whenever we cause a disturbance they have to stand by for a couple more hours. It's just one way of paying them back for all the shit we have to put up with!"

The noise continued, louder and louder until it seemed like it could get no louder.

Now there was a loud thumping sound; the inmates were lifting their beds up and slamming them down on the concrete floor. I heard someone running down stairs, keys jingling, and someone shouting orders. "Cover the second floor, Johnson; stand by the water hose, Clark, just in case."

"They go through all these changes whenever we raise hell. You should take a look at the procedure manual for officers. You'd never believe all the junk they have in there. We really put them in a bind when we steal spoons from the mess hall. You know they have to count the spoons after every meal, and if they're not all there they have to find them?"

"So what's the big deal about a spoon?"

"I'm telling you, man, these hacks are out of their damn minds, they are so scared of us. They think whenever a spoon is missing we are making knives to stick in them!"

"Why don't you just steal the knives if you want to get them upset?"

"What knives? You only get spoons in this joint, man, one spoon, one tray, that's all. They feed you like pigs here, man!"

The noise continued. Now there were shouting voices, threats: "You're going to die, Johnson. First chance I get, I'm going to cut your motherfucking throat! You big dumb bastard! You're too stupid to do anything but turn keys all day!"

"Shut up, faggot!"

"Man, why don't you stop that goddamn noise so I can go to sleep!"

"You should have slept when you were in the streets, punk!"

"I did, with your mother!"

These spontaneous remarks came from different directions, mixed with laughter from the rest of the inmates. It sounded like a great big party!

The big iron gates at the end of the tiers were being opened. The noise and yelling stopped, as if on cue from some unknown source. The guards were patrolling the tiers. It seemed like a show of force. They passed the cell I was in, big, huge monsters of men. I'd never seen men so huge. The only sound you could hear was jingling keys as the guards walked down the tiers. For approximately ten minutes they walked back and forth down the tiers. Suddenly the intercom came on with its count report.

"Attention all units, the count is not clear, the count is not clear. All units make a recount, make a recount!"

The inmates responded with a loud cheer. Again the cell block was in an uproar, the yelling continued: "Make a recount, you big stupid ape!" "Use your toes this time, faggot." "Count your ass off, dodo." These remarks were followed by jeers, loud laughter, beds being slammed against the floor; in victory they yelled. The guards regrouped at the end of the tier and started counting again. It seemed so stupid to watch four men walk down the tier counting. There couldn't be more than thirty inmates on the tier, two men in each cell!

What could be so difficult about that? The counting lasted approximately twenty-five minutes— I could hear the count being called in.

"CB 2, 207!" I was suddenly startled to be able to hear the call. The quietness was deafening. Was everyone listening? It seemed so!

We waited silently for the next count report. Fifteen minutes passed. Half an hour. John broke the silence.

"The count won't clear. Whenever it takes over ten minutes, it won't clear. The guys are probably hiding under their beds. The guards are too damn stupid to realize what's happening."

"The count is not clear. The eleven-thirty count is not clear. Make a recount. All units make a recount."

Another round of applause!

"Yeah, yeah, yeah!"

"Count your fuckin' ass off, Sarge. You big dumb bastard. You can't count your way out of the kindergarten, punk."

This time all the lights came on. Again they counted. The guards looked under the beds. Then they patrolled the tiers again to keep the noise down. We waited for the count report.

At this point, it occurred to me that within these walls were two definite opposing forces—inmates and guards. You were either an inmate or a guard, that's all. Definitely no in-between. I got the impression that it would be necessary to openly oppose the guards to be accepted by the inmates. I was not wrong!

After about ten minutes, the loudspeaker barked: "The count is clear, all units. The count is clear."

There was the sound of commotion as the guards began

to leave the cell block. The large iron gates were being closed and locked. We were all accounted for. Now they would permit us to make all the noise we wanted to.

Again the quietness came, but sleep continued to elude me. Little did I know that this incident was one small example of the animosity and hate that the inmates felt for the guards, nor did I realize that I was going to become a big part of it. For even now, my first night in jail, I was beginning to think in terms of "we" and "they."

I wanted to participate, to demonstrate, to rebel, to strike back at someone, something.

Again I was aware of how tired I was. I began to drift into what I hoped would be a coma. I wanted to close my mind to reality, leave my body and seek sanctuary in infinity, without concern, without fear, without pain, without bars, without counts or recounts. I would rather not face tomorrow. Tomorrow brings a new day and the necessity to deal with my situation. I had one last thought before falling asleep: "If I wake up, I'll deal with it. If not, to hell with it!"

I was awakened by the sound of keys being raked against the iron bars, and a loud voice, "All right, wake up." Get them bunks made. Chow time." The guard raked the keys against the front of our cell. I ignored him and crawled deeper into the sheets. He passed and went all the way down the tier. I tried to go back to sleep. It seemed as if I had just dozed off for a few minutes, but I had obviously slept through the night. I could hear John getting out of the bed and putting his clothes on. The sound of running water soon followed. The guard was on the way back down the tier. This time his voice sounded angry and full of authority.

"Didn't you hear me say get out of that bed? Hey! Wake up in there and make that bed up! Get a move on it, I ain't got all day to be fuckin' with you."

I listened. I was certain that I heard him say, "Get up and

make the bed up." I wondered what time it was. I pushed the covers from over my head and asked John what time it was.

"About five o'clock, man."

"Five o'clock?"

"Yeah."

I crawled back under the covers and lay there, hoping the guard wouldn't notice me but just keep going.

No such luck!

I felt the bed shake violently and he said, "Get the hell up out of that bed, buddy. It's chow time."

I ignored him.

"Hey, get up and make that bed up."

The covers were pulled from me and I snatched my head up and yelled: "Get up for what? I ain't going no goddamn where."

He seemed startled for a second and unable to speak. "You going in the hole if you don't get up out of that bed!"

"Come on and make your bed up, Eddie," said John. "He's just foolish enough to put you in the hole for nothing. You can lay back down after you make it up."

I was so mad I jumped down from the bunk with the intention of snatching the blanket from his hand. Instead, when I jumped from the bunk I was hit with a terrific pain in my side. I screamed in pain and almost fainted. Somehow I managed to hold onto the bars to keep from falling to the floor.

"What's wrong, man? You all right?"

I couldn't speak. John continued: "You can see the man is sick, officer. What the hell you want him to do?"

"Put him in the bed. He'll be all right."

John lifted me back up on the bed and threw the covers on me.

The guard said, "If he's sick you'd better put his name on sick call tomorrow so he can see the doctor Tuesday."

He moved on down the tier waking up the inmates. I felt

like I was going to die from the pain in my side. I'd had
a rib cracked before; it was numb when it happened, but
the following morning was hell! I looked toward the window. It was pitch dark outside. What was all this madness
about eating breakfast and making beds at five o'clock in
the morning? Everybody here must be insanc!

"All right, watch your hands. Coming out. Chow time."

The door slowly rolled open and the inmates began to
step out of their cells. John stepped out onto the tier and
stood in line against the wire mesh screen on the other side
of it. The gate was opened at the end of thc tier and the
inmates began to move towards it. I looked out at them
from my bunk and was surprised that I recognized quite
a few of them.

"Hey, Eddie, when did you get busted, man?"

"I came in last night."

"I'll see you after chow if we have upstairs recreation."

"Yeah, okay!"

After breakfast, John and I talked about the streets. He
was starved for information concerning the "free world."
He appeared to be seeking some assurance that it was still
there. I told him everything I could about the people we
both knew and assured him that they were still doing the
same things.

Listening to him talk, I realized that John had changed
quite a bit. He didn't seem to be the same person that I
once knew. I couldn't put my finger on it. He used to be
indifferent about almost everything. He was a typical
"street hustler." Crime was his way of life. He committed
crimes for a living and tried his best not to get caught. If
he did get caught, he would get the best lawyer he could.
"Best" didn't mean the most expensive or the best by reputation or integrity. Quite the opposite. "Best" was the lawyer who could get the charges dismissed or who could make
a deal with the D.A.'s office to let him plead guilty to a
lesser charge, a charge that he wasn't even guilty of! "Best"

was knowing which D.A.'s would give up a case to win another case. "Best" was winning a case or getting a guilty person off the hook with the least jail term at any cost. John would go to jail gladly for sixty days or ninety days on a charge that carried five to fifteen years, serve his time, and return to the streets and his profession. This was his way of life. Going to jail was an occupational hazard and he accepted it as such.

While in jail he served his time as easily as possible, which meant getting a nice easy job, staying as far away from the guards as possible, and not being involved with the general inmate problems or concerned with prison life in any way.

John would never be involved in riots or prisoner-inspired rebellions, even if the inmates were justified! He wouldn't become involved because it would make his "time hard" and would mean going to the hole, being placed in maximum security units, not receiving visitors or mail. This had always been John's attitude.

But this was not the same person that I was in the cell with now. Still I couldn't tell what was so different—his attitude, yes, but it was more than that.

For one thing, he was extremely bitter and hostile. He separated the world into two categories—those who were "for him" and those against him.

The guards were in the latter category. According to John they were a bunch of sadistic motherfuckers who hated inmates and took all their frustrations out on them. The guards couldn't be trusted in any way. John told me not to trust the guards or anyone else about my case. He firmly convinced me not to believe them or talk to them. He said that I should lie as much as possible in order to confuse the records. I asked him why? He said they would use the jail records against me in court and it would be to my advantage to make the records as inconsistent as possible! His reasoning made sense to me and I vowed to remember all that he told me. Especially about not trusting the guards. We talked on and on about the "streets" as though we were in another world . . . and we were!

I asked John about the jail "schedule" and got a chuckle in reply.

"What damn schedule? You stay in this goddamn cell until they let you out! That's the schedule!"

I couldn't help laughing myself; his remark seemed very funny. I jumped up on the top bunk and lay there smoking a cigarette. An inmate came by the cell and pushed a broom through the bars yelling, "All right, clean-up time."

I took the broom and swept the cell out. Shortly he returned with a wet soggy mop and I jumped down again to mop the floor. After doing what I considered a beautiful job on the floor and getting back on the bed, another fellow came by with a bucket of water and a toilet brush. He asked me if I wanted to clean the commode and I replied, "Yeah, okay!"

After all the housecleaning, I stood there and thought about all the things that John and I had talked about. I was very confused. All of a sudden, a question appeared in my mind. "What the hell am I doing in here?"

Standing there, my knees became weak. I leaned against the bars, closed my eyes, and tried desperately not to cry! I closed my hands around the hard cold bars and clenched my fists as tight as I could. My whole body went rigid and I shuddered. I thought, hoped, prayed, that somehow the force of my body against the bars would shatter this horrible illusion and I would be home again.

The moment was shattered, but my prayers were not answered. John asked me what was the matter? I didn't realize that I had been shaking the door, nor did I realize I was crying—tears of hopeless frustration and fear.

John said, "Take it easy, Jack. They may open the doors for upstairs recreation in a little while and you can get out of this damn cell for an hour."

I wanted to just collapse on the floor in complete defeat.

John must have sensed my feelings. He said: "Keep your chin up, Jack, you can't let these suckers beat you. You've got to fight all the way. Even if you know you can't win, you've got to fight back! They'll kill you if you let them. Ain't nobody going to help you, man. If you don't fight, you can forget it because that will make it all the easier for them to kill you. Look, man, I can't tell you how to serve your time but if you crack up it's all over, you're through bookin'. You've got to get your head together and fight these motherfuckers till you win!"

I was to learn that his words had meaning, especially for me, but right now they were just empty words. . . .

A little while later the inmates began to yell. "Hey Sarge!" "When you going to open these goddamn cells?" "Upstairs rec!" "Open the doors!" The chant went on, accompanied by the tin cups being banged on the bars.

"Rec! Rec! Rec! Rec!"

The whole thing seemed very stupid to me. It appeared that the best way not to be let out of the cells was to cause a disturbance! I asked John about it and he said it was too late for recreation and they were just going to raise a little hell because they didn't get it. He explained that there was just one chance during the day for recreation and if the officer in charge didn't let the inmates out then, they would just have to wait until the next day. I got the impression that there was a huge recreation area full of athletic equipment where the inmates could exercise their bodies and relieve the ever-present anxiety and tension of being confined in a cell all day long. I could readily understand why the inmates wanted to be out of the cells for even a brief moment. I had been in this cell for approximately fifteen hours, and although most of the time was spent sleeping, I could feel the closeness of it and the horrible feeling of being caged. In your wildest nightmare you could never imagine the feeling that accompanies being locked in a cage!

Then it was time for lunch and the cells were opened. The inmates spilled out and stood against the wire fence. John and I stepped onto the tier just as the doors were being closed. The long bar that locks the gate at the end of the tier was pulled and the men went single file down the steps to the dining area. Meals were served cafeteria style. All the food was placed on a long table and the men went by and took whatever they wanted.

Standing in line, I looked out into the dining hall. The men were seated in rows, five men to a row. The tables were simply long steel benches. A guard patrolled the area and maintained complete silence during the meal. I took a little food and walked down the long aisle to the next empty row of seats. John and I were together and we ate quickly and quietly.

After we finished eating, the guard ordered us to pass the spoons to the end of the table. He counted the spoons and dismissed the men one row at a time. He approached our row and looked down the table. I had a little food left on my tray and he ordered me to eat it! I told him that I didn't want any more to eat and he looked at me in disbelief.

"Eat it!" he commanded.

"Go ahead and eat it, Eddie. He'll put you in the hole if you don't."

I ate the food!

Our row was dismissed and we went back to the cell.

"Be careful, Eddie. They will label you a troublemaker and make it hard for you. Just take it easy until you find out what's happening."

Our cell was opened and we stepped in. The inmate that works outside on the tier came by and I got a "telephone request form" from him. I filled out the form to make a call to my mother. I told her that I was in jail charged with housebreaking and traffic. I told her about the time I had received for the traffic offenses and that I was being held on a $5,000 bond on the housebreaking charge. I also found room on the form to tell her not to worry about me! I made out two other telephone requests, one to my brother and one to my girl friend. They had basically the same message. Messages from jail to the three most dearly loved persons in the world. Not a very welcome message, but necessary. No one knew that I was in jail, and it hurt like hell to have to tell them.

On March 20, 1960, two days after I had been in jail, things began to happen. The tier man came to my cell and told me that I had a visitor in the rotunda. My cell was opened and I walked down the tier toward the steps. I was conducted through an endless series of locked cages until I arrived in a huge room with two long tables on opposite sides. Inmates were being interviewed by lawyers and policemen. The guard asked me if I was Eddie Harrison and I replied yes!

"Step up to the table and sign the piece of paper!"

I did as I was told. I didn't know what to expect but I was beginning to get frightened. I had every reason to be. I was told to step inside a room at the end of the rotunda.

Orson White and Ray Sampson were seated there, surrounded by policemen. I was totally unprepared for what I saw. They had both been beaten very badly! Orson's eyes were swollen. He looked angry and also very tired. I could imagine what had happened to him. My own nightmare with the police told me the complete story. It was very doubtful if he had been permitted to sleep the entire time he was in custody.

He looked at me and I read his expression immediately: *"Danger."*

Sampson looked even worse. His eyes were also swollen and his lip was busted. A faint trace of dried blood was on his shirt. The uncertainty vanished. I knew why I was here.

The silence was broken. One of the men in the room spoke.

"Tell him what you told us, Sampson!"

I looked at Sampson but he said nothing.

"Speak up, boy."

Still no word came from Sampson.

"Come with me!"

I was grabbed roughly by the arm and hurried out of the room, to the far end of the rotunda, and told to have a seat. Two men sat at the table in front of me and began to talk. One was black and reminded me of the detective who had nearly killed me in the precinct. The one doing the talking was white and seemingly very nice.

"Look, son, we are here to help you. Sampson told us all about it, so why don't you tell us about it? . . . Here is his written statement. If you want to read it, you'll get a chance to. . . . It will be a lot better for you if you tell us about it. . . . I won't let anything happen to you, son, I promise."

I was afraid to utter a sound. He continued: "You don't believe me, huh? Well, listen to this. Sampson told us that the three of you went to Cider's house to rob him and you killed him! He said he saw you, boy, and he will go to court and tell the judge the same thing. Now, if that's not true, you would be very stupid to let him get away with a thing like that! He's trying to put all the blame on you! Now come on and tell us about it so we can help you."

I wanted to tell him but I couldn't. I was just too damn scared! I knew he was lying in the first place. Sampson couldn't have told him anything like that because it wasn't true, and besides I didn't trust him because he was a policeman and he couldn't have wanted to help me.

He continued: "Look, boy, Stanley Stevenson even told us the same thing. Why don't you be smart and and tell us what happened?"

Still no response from me.

The white officer looked at the black officer as if on cue, and the black one said he was going to get some paper. He got up and left the table. The white officer then turned to me and twisted my arm.

"All right, nigger, if you don't tell me what happened I'm going to take you to the hole and beat your goddamn brains out. I'm tired of fuckin' around with you. When he comes back with that paper, you'd better tell us what happened or we'll beat the shit out of you!"

The pressure on my arm increased; I thought he'd break it, and I was too scared to scream. As suddenly as it happened, it was over, but it was a job well done. I had to tell him or he would do exactly as he said.

The other officer returned and looked at me with an evil grin on his face—a grin that said, "We've got your ass now." I wanted to look to him for sympathy. We were both black and somehow it seemed to me that that alone should be worth something. It wasn't! He only grinned and said: "Start talking, boy. Where's the gun?"

I replied in a meek, scared voice, "I threw it away."

"Where did you throw it?"

"In the trash can."

"What trash can?"

"In my backyard."

"On Fourth Street?"

"Yes, sir."

"Start at the beginning. When did you plan to rob Cider Brown?"

"I didn't plan to rob Cider."

"Don't lie to me, nigger. When did you plan to rob Cider? Was it in R. C.'s?"

"I didn't plan to rob Cider anywhere."

"Sampson already gave us the story. You planned to rob him, didn't you?"

"NO!"

"Goddamn it, boy, I'm going to beat the hell out of you if you lie to me one more time. Didn't you plan to rob him with Sampson and White?"

I dared not answer for fear he would carry out his threat, so I put my head down and looked at the floor.

"Now, that's better. After we type your statement up and you sign it, you can go back to your cell. Okay, start at the beginning and no lies this time."

What lies was he talking about? If I had known what he wanted me to say, I would have said it just to make him go away.

I told him about going to Cider's house to pawn the shotgun and all the events that happened there. I told him about Orson coming into the vestibule and Cider slamming the door and causing the gun to discharge. I told him everything I could remember.

While I was talking, they were taking notes. Afterward, the black officer said that he was going to go and type up the statement. Somehow I felt relieved after telling the story to the officers. I relaxed and waited for the statement to be typed. It only took about ten minutes. He returned and gave a paper to the other officer, who pushed it across the table and held his hand over the typing so that I couldn't read it.

He pointed to a line at the bottom of the paper and said, "Sign it right there."

I asked if I could read it and he replied, "Just sign the paper on that line, boy."

At that moment, Sampson and White were being escorted out of the little room, and it was a timely reminder that I should sign the paper. I took the pen and signed.

Sighs of relief were evident in the two officers, and they called another officer over to the table and told him they were finished with me.

I was taken back into the cell block. I couldn't comprehend the meaning of the police interview or why they were so convinced that I had tried to rob Cider George, but at this point it didn't seem important. They were gone and I was out of immediate danger of being beaten again.

One thing I did know: I was in deep, serious trouble!

I went back to my cell and told John what had happened.

"You damn fool! Did you really sign a statement from the police without reading it?"

"Yeah. I didn't have any choice, man. They were going to take me to the hole!"

"Going to the hole beats the hell outa going to the electric chair, man! That statement could have said anything and you signed it. You've got a lot to learn, man, if you're going to beat this charge. Well, there's nothing you can do about it now. You'd better tell your lawyer about it as soon as possible. Are you going to upstairs rec this afternoon?"

"Yeah, I guess so."

I began to wonder when I would see my lawyer so that I could tell him everything that had happened. I was really beginning to realize that I had done a stupid thing.

When the officer let us out for recreation, we went upstairs. The recreation area was nothing like I had expected, simply a large bare room with a dirty commode in the corner.

The only recreation was walking from one end of the room to the other. I had also found out the reason "recreation" was so important to the inmates. This was the time when the guys could talk to each other about their cases: this was the all-important opportunity for co-defendants to "get their stories together" or for the jailhouse lawyers to get new clients and collect cigarettes from old clients. Some of the inmates did try to have some form of recreation— playing checkers or cards—but most of them just walked up and down the room like caged animals. I talked to some of the fellows that I knew and they were full of questions about the free world. All the questions that John had asked were being asked again. Everyone wanted to know when I came in and what I was busted for.

I had questions, too. I found out that most of the fellows were charged with robbery or murder, and also that most of them were not really concerned about the charges. They talked about getting three to nine years in prison if they were lucky. They talked about the judges they wanted to try their cases and the lawyers they would get. They also talked about which prisons they wanted to go to! They talked about the guards they wanted to beat up or meet in the street on equal grounds. This recreation period was really a community meeting hall.

I noticed a group of guys who seemed to keep themselves apart from the others. Even though they wore the same rough-dry blue jeans and blue shirts, they were quite distinct from the rest of the inmates. They were gathered together in a circle listening to a speaker in the center. The men stood very rigid, arms crossed, and very attentive. I couldn't hear what the speaker was saying, but he appeared to be some kind of preacher or teacher.

Soon the guard yelled, "All right, going back!"

The inmates slowly began to leave the area. I lingered behind to catch a few words from the speaker in the circle.

"All right, Brothers, let's go back to our cells. We must obey this white man's rule as long as we are in his country; but remember, if his rule conflicts with the teachings of Almighty Allah, then we must obey the teachings of Allah. May the blessings of Allah be upon you. As-Salaam-Alaikum!"

The circle responded, "Wa-Alaikum-Salaam."

The strange language was obviously some kind of farewell, but I didn't understand the meaning. After being dismissed, the men turned to each other, shook hands and embraced. Seeing men embrace seemed all the more strange. I shrugged my shoulders, walked down the steps to the third floor, and stood in front of my cell.

The doors were being opened and the men stepped forward. As they were doing so a guy rushed out of the cell next to mine and hurried down the tier. He mingled with the other inmates and disappeared into one of the other cells. John explained that there was a faggot in the cell next to us and the other guy went in his cell during the rec period because the guard had to remain upstairs and supervise. John said that the known homos were kept segregated from the general population, but once in a while one would slip through the screening process and "do his thing" until they caught up with him.

"The screening process?"

"Well, it ain't really a process you know. Most of the punks come in with 'drags' on and they just put them with the rest of the sissies. It's hard to tell who they are if they don't have on drags, unless they are known sissies—that's all there is to it. The hacks really don't give a damn anyway. Man, they don't care who gets fucked as long as it ain't them. They should put all the sissies in general population; that way it would keep the weight off the young boys. But you know what? They don't give a shit about the young boys either."

I asked John about the guys upstairs who were standing in the circle.

"They are the Muslims. Stay away from them, man. They ain't nothing but trouble!"

"Why?"

"Why! Don't you know what the Muslims are? They cause a lot of trouble and always go to the hole for nothing. You already in enough trouble, man!"

"Yeah, but what do they go to the hole for?"

"The guards don't like them and the inmates don't like them. They just cause a lot of trouble!"

"You already said that, but why?"

"Look, man, why don't you talk to them and find out for yourself?"

That made sense. I decided that I would check them out!

The conversation died and I tried to think of something to do. I had read stories of men in jail and I was somewhat amused to find myself doing something that I thought utterly ridiculous—I was unaware that I had begun to count the concrete slabs in the floor! I saw no reason not to and there was nothing else to do so I consciously began to count them! My game soon ended and I still had nothing to do so I tried to talk to John again.

I wanted to find out something—what it was about him that was so different.

"Hey, man, what kinda charge you got?"

"Possession of narcotics, housebreaking, assault on a police officer, and resisting arrest!"

"Wow! Do you think you can beat them?"

"Not if we go to trial. My lawyer is trying to get me a cop-out to the possession charge. Them motherfuckers loaded me up, man; ain't no way in hell I should have all them goddamn charges. You know where the Dunbar Hotel is? Well, I got ten pills from Jimmy Green and went up to the Dunbar to 'take off' in the bathroom. Somebody had moved my works and I didn't have any more so I went down on the first floor to get some works from Petey, but nobody answered the door. I knew the works were in there so I jimmied the door and went in. Somebody must have seen me and called the rollers, but I didn't know it so I went inside and shot the dope. I had three pills left cause the stuff was decent, you know. While I was sitting there nodding, the rollers kicked the door in and busted me. I didn't even know they was cops until I got down to the lock-up. I still had the spike in my arm when they came in and one of them chumps jammed the spike in my arm, man, right through the vein. He just wanted to hurt me, man. I got a long scar on my arm to prove it. Anyway, when he jammed the spike in my arm I went off and tried to kick him in his dick but they jumped me and beat my ass. If I wasn't high they probably would have killed me. I know they would have killed me if I had a gun on me, but I didn't."

John began to get very excited as he was talking. His

anger and bitterness became very apparent. He got up from the bed and continued.

"Man, let me tell you one thing. You see all them motherfuckin' charges I got—possession carries ten years cause it's my second beef—housebreaking carries five to fifteen years—assault on a police officer carries ten years and resisting arrest carries a ball. That's thirty-six goddamn years, man, and if I don't get a cop, I'll probably get every one of them. You know the goddamn police gonna lie their ass off when they go to court, especially on the assault charge. They damn near killed me and I'm charged with assault. Ain't that a bitch? You can bet one thing, though. If them motherfuckers give me thirty years for some shit like that, they gonna have trouble outa me. Man, I'll be ready to die right in that courtroom. I ain't gonna let them bastards railroad me, man. The only charge I should have is the possession charge—three pills, man, *three motherfuckin' lousy pills!* I can do time, man, but they gonna have to shoot me if they try to give me thirty years for this bullshit!"

I could see why John was angry and I could see why he was upset and I knew why he was different. But the one thing that struck me at this point was, if he was in so much trouble because of three pills, where did that leave me charged with a housebreaking that I knew absolutely nothing about and a murder charge in the mail?

There had to be some very serious implications, but I was completely unaware of them. To begin with, I knew that I hadn't broken into anyone's house, and I damn sure didn't murder anyone. I wasn't guilty of any of these things. Wasn't I right in not being overly concerned? Didn't the fact that I wasn't guilty of any of these things make a difference?

Besides, I had already been to court and received my time and it was probably just a matter of going to court and having the judge drop the charges when I tell him what happened! Or I probably wouldn't have to go to court at all; the District Attorney would probably dismiss the charges. After all I just wasn't guilty so what choice did he have? I was beginning to feel very good about the whole thing when John answered the questions I was thinking about!

"You know, man, they don't even give a shit whether you are guilty or innocent. All they want to do is get niggers off the streets any way they can; it don't make no difference if you ain't guilty. If the D.A. thinks he can get you convicted, you're in trouble, man, 'cause all he cares about is getting convictions to make his record look good, and if you're black, you're guilty as hell to begin with—the D.A. just wants to make sure he wins as many cases as he can so he can get to be a judge. All them damn judges used to be prosecutors, man, and they help their friends by making sure they get convictions. The better his record is, the better chance he's got to be a judge! Them is politics, man, and we ain't nothing but a steppin' stone for them. I'm gonna tell you something else, man. Justice in this country ain't shit! It ain't even spelled the same way. Justice is for the white man and he means 'just-us' when he talks about it! When he talks about giving us justice, he means 'just-ice' and that's what you get, baby!"

I was sure that John was just bitter and confused about the whole thing. It couldn't possibly be that way—justice was for all people, not just a handful. He was right about some things. I knew how the police treated people; for the most part, they were a bunch of dirty no-good bastards, but in court was different. I had just come out of school and I knew all about the judicial process and the court system. I had been taught that the purpose of the court was to find the truth and administer justice. I believed in justice and the theory of democracy, and John just didn't know what the hell he was talking about! A lot of things were bad and wrong but it wasn't that bad! From my education, I believed in the Constitution of the United States and the whole theory of having a trial by jury.

While in school I had watched a trial with the rest of my class. I remembered that I was impressed by it. I remembered going into the courtroom and being scared as hell to begin with, afraid to even breathe. The courtroom was very quiet and very cold. Everything was big and impressive—the tables, the desks, the jury box, and especially the bench where the judge sat. I remember being overwhelmed by the sense of power and authority. I remembered all of these things, even down to the seal of the United States and the American flag. Everything about the court was the personification of Power, Wisdom, and Justice. The singleness of purpose, even the fact that there was only one judge behind the bench, impressed upon me the fact that when all was considered, there would be only Justice left.

I decided not to argue these points with John because he obviously had his mind made up. There were just too many parts to the total picture and he had every right to feel the way he did. I came from the same social climate that he did; our backgrounds were basically the same; our outlook was undoubtedly shaped by the same factors but there was a difference. He was much older than I was and much more cynical. I had always had a basic belief in humanity and a tremendous sense of justice, even though I had a very difficult childhood and numerous involvements with the law. As a child I had been put on probation for violations of the law and even sent to reform school after repeated violations—all perfectly just, because I had broken the law. What should I have expected? I held no animosity. I had committed a crime and when you commit a crime, you usually go to jail! Even now, I wasn't bitter because I had been sentenced to ninety days in jail. I was guilty! I was concerned because I had been charged with the housebreaking, but that was a different matter—the housebreaking charge was simply a holding mechanism.

There was no doubt that the charge would be dropped! Even the murder charge. At first even the thought of it scared the hell out of me, but now that I was involved I was sure that they would eventually find out the truth and drop it. They had to!

It was time for the three-thirty count and the guards came past the cell with their pencils and note pads. The count went smoothly. Afterward it would be time for dinner so the inmates didn't bother to cause any trouble. It took ten minutes for the count to clear and the food cart was brought into the cell block.

The inmates who served the food were housed on the first tier. They were let out of their cells and began to set up the dining room for dinner. It was considered a privilege to be a "detail man." Those were the guys who did the work in the cell block. In exchange for their labors, they were permitted to stay out of their cells during the daytime. They served the food, pushed brooms into the cells, and ran errands. The high echelon of the detail men were the cell block clerks and the head detail men—there were two of each. The head detail man was in charge of the other detail men and kept them in line. The inmate clerks, for all practical purposes, ran the cell block, almost every function. They were the only inmates who were permitted to leave the cell block and go to the various other units.

The dining area was soon set up for dinner and the doors were opened. Dinner consisted of fried pork chops, string beans with bacon, sweet potatoes, coffee, and bread. The food smelled very good and my appetite was climbing. Finally, our tier was let out to dinner and the men streamed down the stairs. I was near the end of the line and we were backed up the stairway. John and I sat on the steps to wait for the line to move. We seemed to be waiting an unusually long time and I was getting hungrier by the minute. Still we waited . . .

Finally, I went up ahead to see what the hold-up was. There was some commotion at the serving point. The guy who had conducted the Muslim meeting during the recreation hour was arguing with the guard. He was saying: "We refuse to move until some other type of food is served; you devils know that we do not eat swine or food that is poisoned with swine; yet you continue to serve it!"

The officer, white, around fifty years old and comparatively small, was smoking a cigarette and trying to look calm and at ease. He responded: "Look, buddy, I'm not responsible for what is served on the line; if you want to eat, then go ahead. If you don't, it's all right with me!"

"First of all, I'm not your buddy, devil. Secondly, if you are not responsible, then call the person who is responsible, because we are not going to move until you bring something that we can eat!"

The officer seemed almost apologetic. "Okay, first go and have a seat so the rest of the men can eat, and I'll call the lieutenant so you can talk to him, all right?"

"No! That's not all right—I know your tricks, devil, and I'll say again that we are not going to move until you get something else to eat in here!"

The officer was worried and outwardly irritated at the Muslim's rebelling. The inmates were watching the officer. He didn't seem to know what to do. He was completely at the mercy of the inmates. He had no weapon, nor could he get out of the dining room, because he had left his keys with the other officer stationed on the other side of the room. Finally he turned and walked to the back of the dining room, calling the other officer to let him out. He was pointing to the Muslim. I went back up the stairs and told John what was happening.

"Shit! Them goddamn Muslims better not start no shit, hungry as I am."

"What's going to happen, man?"

"If they refuse to move or let anyone else eat, they'll

probably call the goon squad and make everybody go back to their cell."

"Without dinner?"

"You're damn right! I told you them simple motherfuckers wasn't nothing but troublemakers!"

"What's the guy's name that was holding the Muslim meeting upstairs?"

"Brother Fulwood."

"Is that who's holding the line up?"

"Yeah!"

"Do you know him?"

"Yeah, he used to be a damn good hustler until he got hooked up with the Muslims; now he's the leader and all of them follow him. He's going to start some shit now."

I didn't really understand what was going on. First of all, I didn't see a damn thing wrong with the food. In fact, I liked pork chops, string beans, and sweet potatoes. Secondly, I was hungry as hell. Pork and beans would have been all right with me.

Finally the captain came into the cell block with ten or fifteen officers. The lieutenant came down the first tier; the other officers tagged along behind him. The lieutenant was a big man, white and rednecked. Everything about his manner spoke of authority, even the way he walked! As he approached he swung a huge ring of keys against the side of his leg: his steps were measured and he was obviously aware of the fact that he was being watched by the rest of the men. He did not come into the dining room but stood on the tier, which was enclosed by a thick wire mesh screen. He called Fulwood over to the screen and spoke to him there.

"What seems to be the trouble, Fulwood?"

"The 'trouble' is that we haven't eaten for three days because the food is infested with swine flesh and we refuse to move until something is brought in here for us to eat. It's as simple as that."

"Look, Fulwood, you know that we can't have a separate menu for you people. If you don't want to eat what the rest of them eat, then that's your tough luck. If the food doesn't suit you, then don't eat it. We are not going to bring special food in here for you Muslims. Now, either take the food or move aside and let the rest of the men eat!"

"We are not going to move aside. I don't know what you devils are up to, but we are not going to let you starve us to death either. Now you listen to me. If you want to bring your goon squad in here and start some trouble it's all right with us, but if you want to act like intelligent civilized men, that's all right too. All we want is to get some decent, clean food. All we want from you devils is what we are entitled to."

The lieutenant was getting redder and redder as Fulwood talked. His authority was being openly rebelled in front of the inmates and the other guards. He was in a tight situation. The captain told the officer to open the bars—he stepped out into the dining room.

"All right men, if any of you want to eat dinner, come on down and eat. You kitchen men start serving!"

The situation didn't seem resolved at all, but I was hungry and ready to eat. I started down the steps and my arm was grabbed by John. "Don't go down, Eddie, he wants to use the inmates to clear it up for him. Just wait a minute and see what happens."

Other inmates began to move down the steps toward the serving line. The Muslims tried to talk them out of eating, but the inmates moved forward.

Fulwood spoke out angrily.

"Don't you niggers understand what this devil is trying to do? Can't you see that he is using you? Are you niggers so blind, deaf, and dumb that you can't see what is happening? That's what's wrong with you now, that swine has locked your brain and you can't think! The devils are trying to starve us and poison you!"

His efforts were useless. The line started to move again and the Muslims moved aside.

"All right men, let's keep moving."

The other inmates didn't seem to be paying Fulwood or the lieutenant any attention. They got their food and moved on down the aisle.

The lieutenant spoke: "Come with me, Fulwood!"

It was a command. A settlement had been reached. The human desire for food had ended the stalemate.

Fulwood sensed that it was over and followed the lieutenant. But first he made a speech.

"Be steadfast, Brothers, and obey the teachings. Allah will destroy the devils and their helpers in due time! All praise due Allah and his last prophet, the honorable Elijah Muhammad, As-Salaam-Alaikum!"

As Fulwood was leaving, the rest of the Muslims went to the back of the dining area and took seats. Their leader was gone and they appeared to be lost without him.

I was glad the whole thing was over. Besides, I was hungry. There were a lot of extra pork chops that evening and I had my fill. After counting the spoons, the guard dismissed us one row at a time. We returned to our cells and were promptly locked in for the night. It was only five o'clock, but the day was over and we would be in our cells until the following morning.

I wondered what would happen to Fulwood for resisting the officers. I was somehow impressed by the fact that he stood up to them the way he did. He appeared to be totally unafraid of them, especially the lieutenant, even to the point where he openly insulted him by referring to him as a devil, which the lieutenant didn't react to—then!

"What's going to happen to Fulwood, John?"

"What's going to happen to him? They are going to put him in the hole and kick his ass to begin with! Then they are going to lock him up on M.S.U.—that's the maximum security unit. Then them dirty motherfuckers are probably going to get him indicted for trying to start a riot! The lieutenant is a no-good son-of-a-bitch. The only reason he didn't have the goon squad come in the dining room is because he knew all the inmates would stick together when it came down to that and there damn sure would have been trouble, so he just took all that shit from Fulwood until he could get him outa there. Anytime there is trouble in the dining room they have to be very careful, 'cause they could set the whole thing off. Besides, the inmates could use the trays and buckets as weapons and really give them a hard time. It's not over yet; the Muslims are probably going to raise hell tonight. After they feed the other side there is going to be a lot of shit happening."

He was right. The Muslims refused to return to their cells until they were told what had happened to Fulwood. The goon squad thing was repeated and the lieutenant told them that Fulwood was moved to Cell Block 1. The Muslims accepted this and returned to their cells.

That was before the grapevine got the story! Later on that night, the Muslims found out that Fulwood was in the hole with a fractured skull. He had been beaten by one of the captains after he called him a "white, blue-eyed devil." The captain who was on the evening shift was notorious for beating inmates with his keys. Fulwood had been put in the hole with handcuffs on and the captain had gone to the hole to talk to him. This captain was also known not to take any shit from inmates, especially young, black, belligerent niggers. He was from the old school, which meant put 'em in the hole and whip their ass whenever they get outa line.

When the Muslims found out that Fulwood had been beaten, they started to bang their cups on the doors and make noise. Everyone seemed to participate after the noise started and it grew louder and louder. Cups were being thrown down the tiers and water was thrown from the cells through the retaining screens. The situation soon got out of hand. The other inmates who just wanted an opportunity to raise hell began to throw lighted newspapers onto the tiers. More cups and bars of soap were thrown down the tier at the guards. It was very exciting to be experiencing all of the confusion. The guards stood by and watched. There was nothing they could do until the lieutenant arrived with the goon squad.

They arrived in force. The paper burning on the tier was very frightening, because the cell block appeared to be in complete flames. The sissies were screaming like frightened girls.

The dining room door was opened and the lieutenant stepped into the dining room and stood against the wall. "All right, men!" He could be heard faintly above the noise. "Quiet down! You're only going to make things tougher on yourselves by causing a disturbance!"

His statement seemed ridiculous. How could things be tougher? The inmates took advantage of the opportunity to yell insults at him.

"Fuck you, sucker!"

"Kiss my ass, punk!"

"We like it rough!"

"Make it rough on your mother."

More water was thrown from the tier above us and the lieutenant ran like a dog with its tail between its legs to avoid getting wet.

The officers had succeeded in getting the other side of the block quiet and I could hear one of the cells being opened. Shortly, an inmate came into the dining room and spoke to the Muslims.

"As-Salaam-Alaikum."

There was a loud response. "Wa-Alaikum-Salaam."

"This is Brother Ringo. I am going with the devils to see what has happened to our brother. Be peaceful until I return! As-Salaam-Alaikum."

The yelling began to stop and the officers patrolled the

tiers. Several of the detail men came out and removed the burning paper.

"Who is Brother Ringo?"

"He's a captain or lieutenant or something of the Muslims."

"A captain of the Muslims?"

"Yeah, it's sorta like being second in command."

This whole damn thing seemed like something out of a funny book—the inmates causing all kinds of trouble, for little or no reason, and the lieutenant and his goon squad running around like damn fools.

The inmates had the power to disrupt the whole jail. Whenever the daily routine was broken, the guards had to react and the inmates took advantage of this. I had never seen anything so ridiculous.

It took a while for things to quiet down, but gradually the noise ceased. The tier man came down to our cell and told me that I was going to court in the morning but I would not be permitted to take a shower because of the disturbance.

"What am I going to court for?"

"I don't know, man. You'll find out when you get there!"

"Hey, John, I'm going to court in the morning, man. They're probably going to drop those other charges, huh?"

I felt very happy about going to court, mainly because the charges would be dropped before my family found out about them, and also because it meant that I would be getting away from all of this damn confusion for a while. I wanted to jump for joy, to scream out and yell, "I'm going to court, I'm going to court!" Soon all of this would be over and I could go home!

I didn't care about the other inmates, the captain, lieutenant, or anybody else. All I cared about was leaving this damn place! I had been in jail for three days and it seemed like years. I had begun to really get involved in everything, as though it related to me, and it didn't because I was only going to be here for a little while. To hell with walking up and down the floor in the recreation room and all the other shit that was going on in this madhouse. Let John, Fulwood, Ringo, the lieutenant, the goon squad, and all the other idiots worry about it.

II

Court

(*Eddie*)

The following morning at 5:00 A.M. the officer shook my
bed and ordered me to get dressed. Then the cell door was
opened and I was ordered to go to the dining room foɪ
breakfast. There were approximately twenty other inmates
in there eating. I wondered why we had to get up so early.
It only took about twenty minutes for breakfast and
we were taken to the R and D Unit and searched
once again. We were told that we could take cigarettes with
us but could bring nothing back into the jail. After
getting dressed, we waited and waited. The R and D Unit
was very hot. All of us were crowded into one of the wire-
enclosed cages. There was absolutely nothing to do except wait! I was extremely anxious to get out of there
so I paced the floor. Some inmates found places to sit on
the steel benches in the cage; others were asleep on the
benches.

The loudspeaker announced that it was time for the seven-
thirty count and two guards came into the cage to make

their count. We were counted, and about ten minutes later it was announced that the count was not clear and for them to make a recount. The count was repeated and once again a recount was announced!

The inmates began to get a little irritated. They began to yell insults at the guards.

"Can't you count, motherfucker? I'm tired of sitting in this goddamn cage."

"Use your toes, dumb-dumb!"

Finally the count cleared and the inmates gave a cheer.

The absurdity of what was happening began to bug the hell out of me. I wanted to get to court.

I didn't know that I would spend that whole day waiting in a cage in the Juvenile Court, where exactly nothing happened. Late in the evening I was returned on the bus to the D.C. Jail. Too many cases, they said.

I finally got back to my cell around eleven-thirty, and John was asleep. I was thankful for that because I didn't feel like answering any questions. I was very tired.

Why the hell was I called to court? The question kept popping up in my mind. I was so damned disappointed I could have cried! Another night in jail? A week? How long would I be in this madhouse? I went to sleep aching to be free, crying out in my mind, "Let me go! Let me out of here!"

The following day I consciously withdrew from all that was happening around me. John sensed my mood. He didn't speak to me at all. Around seven o'clock the tier man came to my cell and told me that a fellow named Orson White had sent me a message. I took a crumpled piece of paper from him and quickly read the note. Orson and Ray had been admitted to the jail and they were both charged with first-degree murder. The note said that he would talk to me at breakfast the following morning.

If Orson and Ray were charged with first-degree murder, then I sure in hell was! I sent Orson a note telling him not to talk to anyone about it and that I would see him in the morning.

Orson was on the fourth tier and I lingered behind at breakfast so that I could be the last one out from our tier. Orson was the first to come down the steps from his tier and we were able to sit together and talk.

He told me that Ray had voluntarily gone with the police when they came to his house. He told them that he was not involved in the Cider George case. Orson also told me that the police had come to his house and arrested him after thoroughly searching for a "sawed-off shotgun." Orson was taken to the police precinct and confronted with Ray. Ray was then taken into a separate room and questioned again while Orson was being questioned in another room. The police finally ended up with a confession saying that the three of us had gone to Cider George's house to rob him!

"That's what the police were trying to get him to say when they brought us over here the first time. But it's a lie!"

I had shouted, and the other inmates were all looking at me. The guard came to our row and told me that there would be no talking in the dining room. I quieted down and repeated that it was a goddamn lie! Orson told me that Ray said the police had made him sign the statement!

"How in the hell could he sign a statement that wasn't true?"

I was suddenly hit with the realization that it was very easy for him to sign a statement that wasn't true if he didn't read it first!

I quickly told Orson about the statement that the police made me sign without reading and about going to court the day before.

Orson was visibly shaken by what I had told him and I guess he should have been!

Breakfast was over and we went back to our cells. I was to meet Orson at recreation time.

We were in big trouble and the only thing to do at this point was to get out of it.

Ray Sampson was in a different cell block, and the only chance we would get to see him would be when we went to court or were called out to see our lawyers. It was damned important for us to get together so we could all find out what the hell was going on.

I was relieved to find out that we were going to have recreation. I hurried upstairs to meet Orson. He was in a depressed mood. Orson had been in jail before and was more aware of what we were faced with. During our conversation, I found out that the police had beaten him, too, until he agreed to sign a statement. He didn't know exactly what the confession was, but it was a confession.

Bitterness grew within me because of the apparent total lack of regard for the truth. The Police Department had no right to take advantage of us but there was absolutely nothing we could do about it. We were at their mercy, and their only interest was to solve the "Cider George murder case" and bring someone to trial for it as quickly as possible. The police were responsible for gathering anything that could be considered evidence and be used to get a conviction, and they did a damned good job of it!

They obtained evidence to support their theoretical reconstruction of the case and disregarded everything that did not support their theory. We were in deep shit. I could do away with fantasizing about going home and resign myself to the reality of being charged with first-degree murder!

That night I wrote a letter to my mother and explained as best I could that I was charged with first-degree murder and would need a lawyer to defend me. I knew that my family could not afford to hire a lawyer, but that was of no importance. I had to have a lawyer if I was going to get out of this trouble, and I would need the best lawyer money could buy—one who had connections.

The following day the three of us were taken to the coroner's office for an inquest hearing. It was a preview of what would happen at the actual trial, a pre-trial of sorts. The police were there in force. I found out that the two officers who talked to me at the jail were assigned to the Homicide Division of the Police Department and that they were very accomplished liars!

Ray Sampson was the only one who had a lawyer present, and he represented all three of us. L. A. Harris was a trial lawyer. He was black and thin with a lean hard face and an inquisitive glare. He leaned over and instructed us to just sit there and not react to anything that happened.

Sampson had evidently told him about the police. He went on to say, "I know these are a bunch of lying bastards, but don't worry about it. I'll take care of it!" I felt relieved because he was there and knew that the police were a bunch of liars. I liked him right away. His presence alone somehow reassured me and I relaxed.

I looked around to see if any of my family were there. I was glad that they were not, because I had some idea as to what to expect and it wasn't something that I wanted my family to be a part of!

The hearing was very informal, not at all like a regular trial. The coroner testified as to the causes of death. Cider George had met his death as a result of a shotgun blast on March 10, 1960, at approximately 8:15 A.M. The coroner's report should have been a simple statement of his findings, but the report reeked of prejudice and the Police Department's influence. The gory details of the wounds caused the coroner's jury to turn on us with threatening stares.

From his statement alone, we would have been found guilty. His testimony was that Cider George's head was literally torn away from his body by a close-range blast from a 12-gauge shotgun. Death was instantaneous because the brain was completely destroyed. His eyes were also torn from their sockets.

He further testified that the shot traveled upward and had also severed the main artery in the neck, which caused profuse bleeding. He testified as to the contents of his stomach and added that he had obviously not finished eating breakfast! Cider George's nephew was there to identify the body, and his testimony was just about the only truth told in the courtroom! From then on, the whole procedure was a complete farce. The police testified that the three of us were involved in an attempted robbery in which Cider George was murdered. One of the officers who had questioned me testified that all of us had confessed to the murder. The statements were introduced as evidence and passed around to the coroner's jury. Sampson's lawyer did not let any of us testify. We were told to just remain silent and see what else they had.

I was beginning to feel like a pawn in a chess game, about to be sacrificed.

There were other witnesses. Wilma Russell, Stanley's girl friend, testified that she was in Stanley's house when the police first arrested us. She said that she had never seen me before nor did she hear any conversation among the four of us on the morning we were arrested. Her testimony didn't seem important at the time but it was going to prove extremely important later.

The hearing continued with other witnesses being called in to testify. There was a lady who lived directly across the street from Cider who testified that she was cleaning the dresser off in her bedroom when she heard a tremendous explosion. She said that she immediately rushed to her window and saw two men run from Cider's doorway and rush down the street. She said that she could not identify the two men, but one of them was holding a shotgun and trying to push it under his coat!

The only function of the coroner's inquest is to determine the cause of a person's death and decide if there is sufficient evidence to warrant a grand jury hearing. The only evidence to support grand jury disposition was the coerced confessions!

The police had done a beautiful job in writing the confessions. They were constructed to get a conviction of first-degree murder and they were masterpieces. I realized later that they met every legal prerequisite for a felony murder indictment and conviction. They couldn't have been written any better if composed by the judge himself. They were by far the most damning pieces of evidence. They fit together like pieces of a giant puzzle.

The confessions were read and passed around for the members of the jury to read. They were signed, sealed, and being delivered. Hearing the confessions was a hell of a shock. They were lies! Complete lies, goddamn lies!

If I were a member of the coroner's jury, I would have voted guilty! I could hardly contain myself.

The hearing was brief, and the verdict was reached in a matter of seconds. The case was being sent to the Grand Jury and we were ordered held without bond pending their investigation.

Sampson's lawyer promised to visit us in a couple of days and Orson and I were advised to get lawyers and have them get in touch with him. The courtroom quickly cleared and we were handcuffed and taken back to the District Jail.

The process of being recommitted allowed plenty of time to talk among ourselves, and we were able to relate our different experiences with the police, which proved not to be different at all. We had all been the victims of a very old and refined process called "the third degree." I wondered how many others had been subjected to the same treatment! How in the hell could this be happening? It was still hard to believe. We decided that the only thing we could do was to tell the truth and hope that somehow it would prevail!

Since Sampson was the only one with a lawyer at this point, we decided that he would represent all three of us until we could get lawyers. All of us were in very bad moods, especially me. I felt very hostile and angry because of the inquest and was looking for an outlet for my hostility. I found it in R and D as I was being processed back into the jail. We had been sitting naked in a cage, waiting for our names to be called so that we could be searched. It was very cold; there was a huge fan that blew directly through the cage and we could not avoid the stench it circulated; the fan was the first thing that irritated me after I was back in the jail. Then I was called to step forward to be searched. The guard barked orders: "Step up to the line, raise your arms, run your fingers through your hair, open your mouth, lift your balls, bend over and spread your cheeks." I simply stood there with my clothes in my hand and let my anger swell. I gritted my teeth and felt the blood rushing to my head. The guard looked at me, unaware and uncaring about my emotions. He stepped closer to me and shouted directly into my face: "Didn't you hear me? Put those damn clothes down and go through the moves." I balled the clothes up in my hand and threw them in his face. "Fuck you, Police."

I was on the verge of a bigger explosion. I just couldn't keep myself together any longer. It was too much!

One of the inmates ran over and pushed me out of the cage, telling me to take it easy, calm down! Orson came over and talked to me and I sat down on the cold steel bench. The inmate went back into the cage to talk to the guard, who had gone to the phone. He was probably calling the goon squad, but I didn't give a damn. What else could they do to me? The incident was over almost as quickly as it had happened. Others were called for searching and I just sat there.

Orson's name was called and he hesitated in order to see if I was all right before going into the search cage. I nodded to him and he went into the cage. I was beginning to feel the chill, so I doubled up and put my head down on my knees. After everyone else was called, my name came up again and I stepped into the cage again. "All right, young fella, pick those clothes up and let's try it again!" Without even thinking about it, I picked the clothes up and put them on the table.

"Step back and raise your arms." I did so, slowly. The guard seemed to be more patient with me this time; he talked slowly and in a tone of voice usually used to deal with mental patients!

"Open your mouth.

"Run your fingers through your hair.

"Raise your balls.

"Turn around and spread your cheeks."

I followed the instructions and stepped through the line. An inmate handed me my blue jeans as I stepped through.

"Be cool, young boy. You can't win in this joint."

"Yeah, everybody keeps telling me!"

The cell block was quiet when we went in. I went up to the fourth tier with Orson and stood in front of his cell with him.

"Who are you going to get for a lawyer, man?" he asked.

"I don't know. I'll ask my cell partner and see who he thinks is the best. It's going to be up to my family to pay for him."

"What do you think of L. A. Harris? He's a damn good lawyer. Most nigger lawyers are shit because they are afraid of Whitey in the courtroom and they don't have any connections outside of the courtroom. L. A. Harris don't give a damn about them or their connections. He wins his cases on law! Them other lawyers go in there pleading friendship with the judge and the judge don't give them nothing but a hard time! I'm going to get me a white lawyer; somebody who drinks tea with the judge in his chambers."

Orson continued. "I had a lawyer named Goldberg when I got locked up before. He got me off free and I was guilty as hell. I know he can get me off this time because I ain't guilty of nothing!"

"Going back!"

The cell doors began to open and Orson stepped inside. I ran down to the third tier and stood in front of my cell and waited.

The officer came down to my tier, but instead of opening the cell door, he came on to the tier and walked toward me. I sensed that something was wrong.

"What's your name?"

He took out a pad and patted his pocket for a pen.

"Eddie Harrison."

"What were you doing on the fourth tier?"

"I was talking to my friend."

He couldn't find a pen but he continued to search himself.

"Don't let me catch you trembling again or I'll lock your ass up. You understand?"

"What do you mean 'trembling?' "

"Don't let me catch you on another tier, I don't care who you are talking to! Now get in that damn cell!"

He went storming back down the tier and slammed the door. In a few seconds the cell door began to roll open. John had been listening, and he told me that the only thing that kept clodhopper from putting me in the hole was that he didn't have a pen to write me up!

I didn't realize how tired I was from going to the inquest. My body felt drained of all energy. My mind was tired, my tolerance for everything was just about gone.

I wondered why none of my family had visited me. I wanted to see my mother but I was afraid to face her. Afraid because of the pain I knew she would feel. Afraid because I would have no answers to the probing questions and would not be able to explain why I was in jail.

I fell asleep thinking about my mother and what I would say to her when she came to visit me.

The sounds of life in the jail dictated how one was expected to respond. The sound of doors opening was indicative of some type of activity, depending on the time of day. Being blind in jail would not have been a handicap at all. There was no need to see anything. There was nothing to see. The view from my cell was quite typical, on a horizontal plane looking directly at a flaky brick wall.

The tier only allowed for two bodies abreast and there were only two directions in which one could move, to the dining room on one end and to the shower on the other.

The sounds of a door opening, a cart being pushed down the rough cement aisle, pots and pans rumbling as the cart moved down toward the front of the dining room, the gate opening and slamming shut as the detail men came out into the dining room. Heavy thuds as the pots were dropped on the flat steel table which sufficed as a serving table. The stainless steel trays being stacked onto the table.

"Chow time." The signal for all to get ready to be released from their cells.

"Coming out!"

The jingle of huge keys being put into the lock.

Slam! The panel being opened.

Chank, chank. The locks being released.

RRRRRRRRRRR. The crank being turned to release the animals.

Silence as the men stepped out of the cages.

RRRRRRRRRRRR. Bang! The doors being closed.

Slam. The panel being closed.

Jingle, jingle, jingle, jingle. The guard running up the stairs to repeat the same operation on the next tier.

My mother visited me soon after. I went through the routine of being let out of my cell and hurried down the steps to the gate in the dining room. I was searched and permitted to go to the second floor. The visiting area was crowded. I was put into an oblong steel tank with a wire mesh screen overhead. There were chairs facing a steel wall with diamond-shaped glass windows. In front of each chair to the right of each window was a telephone attached to the steel wall. My mother was sitting on the opposite side of one of the windows when I arrived.

She smiled as I sat down and picked up the phone. I was very happy to see her and didn't mind the horrible inhuman condition under which we were seeing each other. Behind the smile I could see pain, anger, and the unmistakable facial expression that told me she was close to tears.

My anxiety about seeing her was justified. I hurriedly started to tell her about the traffic charges and the house-breaking, but neglected to mention anything about the inevitable murder charge. Like most black mothers, she was familiar with troubled times. She had suffered with me through Junior Village when I was ten years old, the receiving home for boys at twelve, and Cedar Knoll School for Boys at fourteen. Now she was prepared to stand by me through this ordeal.

Mothers are strange creatures, protective by nature. She would again attempt to bear the pain of my suffering and challenge everything that threatened me. I told her about the police arresting me and beating me at the station and of the transfer to the jail. The visit lasted for one-half hour. Before leaving, she told me that my girl friend Maxine, who was five months pregnant with my second child, had attempted to visit me but was not permitted to because she was not my legal wife. My mother promised to get a lawyer for me and visit me the following week. She told me not to worry; the Lord makes everything work out for the best. A guard came over and told her that the visit was over and we put our hands against opposite sides of the glass in a farewell gesture. I quickly turned my head as she was leaving so as not to see the tears that I knew would come.

Later on in the week, L. A. Harris visited the three of us. We were very apprehensive and wanted to know what was being done. We learned that the murder charge was before the Grand Jury and we could expect to be indicted within a few weeks. L. A. told us that the government appeared to have a very strong circumstantial case against us. First of all, there was a dead body. Secondly, there were three suspects, all of whom had confessed. Thirdly, there were two eyewitnesses to the crime; and fourth, there was the statement of Benjamin Eugene Valentine, who said I had confessed to the crime in the R. C. Restaurant. It was as simple as ABC, or basic arithmetic: crime plus suspect plus confession equals indictment!

L. A. did most of the talking. He told us quite frankly that we were in deep shit. He told us all the things that we did wrong. He talked as if he were a football coach going over a game that we had lost. He was doing the same damn thing that the police had done, reconstructing what he "thought" had happened. Was this whole fuckin' nightmare a game of some sort? I sat there and listened to all of the things I should have done in order to have successfully robbed and killed Cider George. It was absurd to listen to L. A. talk about a crime that never occurred, but the more I thought about what had actually happened, the more ridiculous everything appeared.

I had not read a newspaper for the last week or so. L. A. had several newspaper articles concerning the "Cider George murder." They were all front page headlines. "THREE NEGROES ARRESTED IN CIDER GEORGE CASE"; "TRIO CONFESS TO CIDER GEORGE MURDER."

I read the newspaper accounts of what had happened and was somehow more shocked because of the untruth. It was obvious where the newspapers got their information and whose side of the story they were reporting.

The stories were not even accurately recounting the police version. They were obviously written by a very dramatic journalist whose purpose was to sell newspapers rather than report the facts.

L. A. was saying: "The first thing we are going to have to do is get a good story and stick to it. Repeat it over and over in your minds until it becomes the truth; write it down, recite it every day, and don't change it, no matter what happens.

"Now I've handled such cases before and I know what's best. I'm a friend of the Kennedys, you know!"

I looked up from the newspaper article and began to pay a little more attention to what he was saying.

"You say you're a friend of the Kennedy family?"

"Well, not a friend of the family. I went to school with Bobby Kennedy and he knows me, so don't worry, I'll take care of this case." He seemed to be very sure of himself so I let it pass.

He continued: "I want all of you to know how important it is for you to stick together. If any one of you gets scared and decides to turn state's evidence in exchange for a light sentence, you're all finished! The government will try to get to you and offer a cop in exchange for your being a government witness, but you'd better make up your mind right now to refuse any such offer if you ever want to get out of jail."

L. A. Harris was right about one thing. I was damn sure scared as hell, but I had no intention of pleading guilty to anything. "We'd better get a story together. Now tell me what happened so we can figure out something."

Orson was saying that he didn't know what had happened. The only thing he knew was what I had told him. Sampson's remark was the same. I told L. A. what had happened from the beginning to the end. As I talked, he shook his head from time to time but did not interrupt me.

I don't know how long I talked; it seemed like a long time. L. A. was taking notes and drawing little diagrams on his pad. When I finished, he shook his head and said I'd have to find another story. He didn't believe it!

I felt betrayed. He went on to say, "If you go into a courtroom with that story, you're going to talk yourself right into jail. I don't care if it is the truth; you are helping the government's case with this story and you'll just have to change it if you're going to testify in your own behalf."

"I don't know what else to say. It's the truth, damn it!"

"It may be the truth. I don't really care if it's the truth. What I care about is winning this case. The government's case is going to be hard to prove and I'm going to make it tougher. You know their theory is that the three of you went there to rob Cider and he was killed! Now Eddie, they say that you were carrying the shotgun because he didn't know you and wouldn't be able to identify you later. Let's start at this point and get our defense together. We are going to have to completely destroy the government's case, piece by piece."

We talked over every angle and gave him the names of possible witnesses for our defense. It was getting late and L. A. had to leave. He promised to visit us the next day and told us not to talk to anyone about the case because the police often sent undercover men into the jail to try and get information for them.

We were also told to write down everything that happened from the time that we met at the R. C. Restaurant up to now and have it for him the following day. We were also told not to consent to interviews with police officers or people from the prosecutor's office.

Later that evening I went over the whole thing again and made notes. John told me about a lawyer he was reading about in the paper; his name was George Thomas and he specialized in murder cases. He had recently won a first-degree murder case in the District Court. I made a mental note to contact him and see if he would take my case.

Time was beginning to pass unnoticed, as though it never were. How very unimportant it seemed that my youth was oozing from my body. Eighteen years old and the most notable occurrences of my life were the daily activities of the D.C. Jail.

Mondays weren't so bad. We were permitted to shower

and shave. I must have had all of ten hairs on my chin and it was kinda nice to pretend to need a shave. Tuesday was sick call day and a lot of fun also. The fun thing about sick call was that you had to prepare for it. The sick list was made the night before, and if your name wasn't on the list you could not see the doctor. If your name was properly put on the list and arrangements were made with your illness to show up the following morning, then you could get your aspirins. Wednesday, visiting day, filled with anxiety and tension. One-half hour with reality and a peep at your wife, mother, daughter, or son. A half hour of deceit, hastily spoken words, and halfhearted promises. Thursday, scrub-down day, one of the good days. A few men were permitted to work—to vent hostility and anger via a scrub brush. Fire hose shooting water over everything and mass confusion. Friday, canteen day, another good day for those who had money in their accounts. A chance to buy cigarettes, toothpaste, soap, or writing paper and stamps. Saturday, weather permitting, outside recreation. The outdoor recreation facilities were almost the same as the indoor facilities—a large empty yard for walking. On Sundays, the Catholics, Protestants, and Salvation Army competed to save the souls of the sinners.

Mass was held in one of the fumigated cages in R and D. The same floors which a few hours earlier received urine, spit, and drunken bodies now received the knees of the faithful in prayer.

Protestant services were held in the dining room and it was impossible to escape the ritualistic Protestant hymns —"The Old Rugged Cross" or "Jesus Keep Me Near the Cross."

The Salvation Army commanded the upstairs recreation area, brass band and all. The bellowing, intruding sound of the tuba was always a sure sign that it was Sunday morning. The Salvation Army always had the largest attendance. You could hardly find standing room at the services.

The three faiths had basically the same thing to offer to the inmates—the word of God, joyous song, and a sympathetic ear, but the Salvation Army had one other thing—women of sorts. The men went to see the women, all of whom were either very old and motherly or very young and sisterly. If we were lucky, one of the young ones played the portable field organ and we could get a glimpse of a partially exposed thigh. The older women were more cooperative but far less exciting. I don't think they ever knew why the men always chose the very fast songs to sing.

The one-sided consummation of the sexual desire generated by the mere presence of the strange sexless women often took place late at night in the semi-privacy of the dark cell.

Such marked the passage of time.

My mother had retained a lawyer for me, Perry W. Howard, a black lawyer whose reputation was for having connections more than being a capable lawyer. He was very much a part of the Washington cocktail set and had influential relatives, including a judge, and his son, a bondsman. I wrote several letters requesting to see him but he always appeared to be busy or didn't have time to come to the jail. He said I would be coming to court soon and he would see me then.

Orson had gotten a lawyer also, and we had talked to him several times. It was decided that our defense would be to rely on the government's not being able to prove its case. After all, how could they prove something that never occurred?

We were finally indicted by the Grand Jury on two counts of first-degree murder—first, murdering Cider George with premeditated malice; second, felony murder. The government had an option; if they couldn't prove one count, they could fall back on the second count. More and more I realized that no one really cared what the truth was except me, and I didn't make a damn bit of difference to anyone.

71

A U.S. marshal came to the jail and personally handed me the indictment papers, a list of the witnesses who would be called to testify against me, and a list of all the jurors. Having the indictment presented to me was the official beginning of the *United States of America* vs. *Eddie M. Harrison.*

The language of the indictment was very intimidating. The power and force of the United States were evident and so was the realization that that power was going to be levied upon me.

I knew a few of the witnesses. More than half of them were police officers. I was surprised to see the name of Stanley Stevenson as a government witness. Stanley was my friend—but so was Benjamin Eugene Valentine.

We were taken before a judge to answer the indictment, and this was the first opportunity I had to talk with my attorney since my mother had retained him. I was very disappointed.

"As your attorney I advise you to plead guilty to second-degree murder. That's the only thing that can save you."

This from the defender of my rights, the champion of justice, as I stood in the cold steel cage waiting to see the judge. I was visibly shaken. Didn't he realize that he was asking me to spend the rest of my life in prison? My very first thought was, "This old baldhead motherfucker must be out of his goddamn mind!"

He hadn't asked me my name. He sensed that I was upset, but he didn't quite have the reason together. His feeble attempt to console me angered me more than I can express.

"Look, son, I know how you feel, but believe me I know what's best. I've been practicing law in this town for fifty years and I'm telling you, the only thing you can do is plead guilty to second-degree murder. I'm sure I can arrange it with the D.A."

This was unreal—the tone of his voice, rough and

throaty, strained as though he were forcing the air from his lungs and pushing it past his vocal cords. An old man, even in appearance, brown baggy suit drooping from his body as only an old man can wear a suit, pants held by wide white suspenders that were only in place when his thumbs were tucked in them. Spectacles on the tip of his nose, but secure enough to just hang there as he peered over the rims. He had the unmistakable air that some old men project of having once been important, the reminiscent trend of thought that's never relevant.

He was saying something but his words had no meaning. I shouted that I wasn't going to plead guilty to a damn thing! Then I tried to speak calmly, to explain how I felt, but nothing came out right. I didn't have my thoughts together. I had expected him to assure me that he was going to get me out of jail somehow, to say something to encourage me, to advise me, to help me.

"If that's what you want to do, boy, we'll go to trial, but we don't have a chance."

He would have been pleased to have me plead guilty. His troubles would be over and mine would be just beginning. He was in for a hell of a surprise. It didn't matter what the consequences were, I was determined to not live the rest of my life in somebody's prison.

Our conversation was interrupted by a marshal. "The judge is getting ready to come on the bench. Take your place in the courtroom."

"All right, son, we'll go to trial!"

We entered the courtroom. I was escorted by two U.S. marshals, who were constantly beside me.

The courtroom was very crowded and there was an air of excitement. I held my head down, only out of fear of looking up.

"All rise. Hear ye, hear ye, hear ye. This honorable court is now in session. Be seated and come to order. Clerk, call the first case."

"The *United States of America* vs. *Eddie M. Harrison.*"

The marshal gently nudged me out of my chair and walked me to a place in front of the judge. There was some commotion as Perry Howard ruffled papers and came to stand beside me. His thumb automatically went to his suspenders.

"If the court please, Your Honor, my name is Perry W. Howard, Sr. I am the attorney for the defendant." The judge simply nodded his head.

The clerk of the court handed the judge a copy of the indictment, which he proceeded to read. "The United States of America charges that on or about March 8, 1960, Eddie M. Harrison, Orson G. White, and Joseph R. Sampson did murder George H. Brown by means of shooting him with a shotgun while attempting to perpetrate the crime of robbery. . . ."

On and on he read. My knees were beginning to get weak and I felt as though I were swaying back and forth. I reached out for something to support myself.

"How do you plead?"

"Not guilty." My voice was weak and strained.

"This matter will be put on the docket for trial."

I was led from the courtroom, and as I walked away, I quickly asked my lawyer to come back to the bullpen to talk to me before he left.

The marshals took me back to the jail before I had a chance to talk to him, but the following day's newspaper accounts provided me with the information I wanted.

"TRIO PLEAD 'NOT GUILTY' IN CIDER GEORGE MURDER"

I had only spoken two words in the courtroom but that was obviously enough for the papers to print a three-column story with pictures.

L. A. Harris visited us frequently during the next few months. He seemed to always be there when we wanted to discuss the case or when we felt something was important or remembered some point or bit of information. He always had encouraging news—some contradictions in the government's case, their not being able to contact the witnesses, or news of someone who was going to appear as a defense witness. L. A. was always enthusiastic about the outcome of the case. He felt that we were going to win with no problem.

Even though L. A. Harris was Sampson's lawyer, I trusted him and had complete confidence in his ability to get us out of this trouble. I wanted to have him for my attorney, but he convinced me to keep Perry Howard on the case because Howard did have certain political and social contacts that might prove to be useful.

Our trial date was nearing and a motion was filed in court to send Orson and me to St. Elizabeth's Hospital for ninety days' mental observation in order to further delay the trial. I had heard rumors about St. E.'s and was looking forward to going there, if for no more reason than to have a vacation from the jail.

III

St. Elizabeth's

(*Eddie*)

St. Elizabeth's is the name of the nuthouse in Washington, D.C. Located in the Anacostia section of Washington, it looks like a nice summer resort area—plenty of green grass in the summer, nice cottages spaciously separated, trees and benches along curved walkways.

The only things that lead one to suspect that it's not what it appears to be are the tall, spiked iron bars that surround it and the uniformed guards at the entrance. I was registered and sent to Ward 5. The facilities there were different, but the procedures were the same as in the D.C. Jail. I was taken to a room and told to strip. I was searched for whatever people in authority look for when they search you and was told a few things about the hospital and more particularly John Howard Pavilion, where I was. After changing clothes, I was taken out onto the ward to meet the head attendant and the nurses.

"This is Mr. Eddie Harrison, a new patient. Mr. Harrison, I'd like for you to meet Mrs. Bryant, the ward nurse, and Mr. Harris, the head attendant."

Harris was friendly. I liked him right away. Mrs. Bryant shook hands with me, unaware of the instant pleasure it gave me to be able to touch her. Harris and I shook hands also, but somehow that didn't turn me on at all. It felt very good to be around real people. This may very well have been the first time anyone had called me Mister. I liked it. I was immediately aware of how very different everything was in comparison to the jail. The first attendant that I met was young, I guess around twenty-two years old, black, and seemingly well educated. So was Harris. The most startling difference, though, was the way I was treated. Like a human being. With a little common decency. It certainly felt good to be away from the tension of the jail.

Sullivan, an attendant I had met earlier when I registered, took me for a tour. There were about twenty-five men on the ward. At eighteen, I think I was probably the youngest. From the looks of some of the others I imagined that they ranged up to eighty. There was a long hallway with private bedrooms at one end. There was constant traffic in the hallway. Some of the men walked very fast as though they were in a hurry to get to the other end and others seemed to be making a tremendous effort to move their feet. I noticed that they all looked like zombies.

Sullivan told me about some of the patients and why they were there. "Lawyer Williams" was a brilliant trial lawyer who allegedly shot and killed a judge for deciding against his client. Williams had been in St. Elizabeth's for thirteen years. He was not competent to stand trial, so he just sat there.

"Jesse James" was so busy running from the sheriff that he didn't have time to go to the bathroom.

"Diamond Jim" always had his pockets filled with rocks, and if he liked you he'd put some under your pillow.

"Sheriff" had paper badges taped all over him. Sheriff was not crazy, though; he knew that the real Jesse James was dead so he didn't have time to fool around with

"Jesse." Besides he had to find out how Diamond Jim was smuggling the diamonds in.

There were the extremists, guys who were playing crazy. Butch Miller, three armed robbery charges, one rape charge, and assault with intent to kill. He'd better be crazy. If he didn't get committed to the hospital, he'd never get out of jail.

I hadn't quite made up my mind about Sullivan, but after we talked for a while, I decided that I liked him.

"Come on, it's time for lunch," he said. We left the porch and went into the hallway, where a line was beginning to form. I stood in line and Sullivan walked on down the hall.

"Hey, mister, do you want to buy some diamonds?"

"Huh?"

"Do you want to buy some diamonds?"

The words were spoken by a strange-looking little man whose hands were cupped in front of him holding something tightly. He moved down the line without waiting for an answer.

One of the men that I noticed earlier walking up and down the hall seemed angry because the line had formed in his path. He continued to walk faster and faster, only this time his head was shaking violently and his arms were raised as if to strike. He stopped occasionally and cursed. "Goddamit, goddamit," he yelled—and reached out and touched the wall. He was coming toward me. Suddenly he stopped directly in front of me and shouted, "Kill the bastards! Kill the bastards!" He raised his hand slowly, trembling and shaking as though he were gathering all the power of his body. His face was distorted in an angry snarl but he merely reached out, touched the wall and moved away. I was prepared to hit him if he had gotten too close to me. I had no way of knowing if he were serious or not, but I damn sure wasn't going to wait too long to find out.

The dining room was a real dining room with chairs and tables. One of the surprising things was that there were knives, forks, and spoons—even napkins, plates, and glasses. It seemed ironic, but the people who were supposed to be crazy were treated like normal people and the people at the jail who were supposed to be normal were treated like they were crazy.

Lunch was served piping hot from a steam table. There were even female waitresses who greeted you. Hell, I was really going to enjoy being in "simple city"!

I sat at a table and was soon joined by two other fellows. We ate in silence.

The remainder of the day was spent just walking around on the ward and on the porch. I wrote letters to my mother and my girl friend.

At the jail I was not permitted to see my girl friend or write to her without special permission, but it would be different here. I looked forward to the day when I would see her.

Sullivan came out on the porch and we talked more about the hospital and the regulations. He also said we would be going outdoors soon for recreation.

Again, contrary to the jail, recreation meant recreation. The recreation yard was huge and full of equipment. There were tennis courts, basketball courts, a baseball diamond, a track, weights, even a garden. I just walked around the yard a few times trying to decide what to do. There was even a small band playing in the yard. "Diamond Jim" was wandering around the garden, probably looking for jewels.

I listened to the band for a while and walked over toward the basketball courts. The attendants were playing the patients. Funny—the patients were way ahead. I waited until the game was over and went out onto the court to shoot a few. We started another game. This time only patients were playing. I like to play basketball but the pace was too much for me. Looked like I blew more than my perspective at the jail.

I somehow got through the game and went out and lay

down on the lawn to cool off. It was nice to lie in the cool grass and feel a light breeze gently blowing over your body—to close your eyes and be totally aware of the wonderful, beautiful, open space around you.

It was even possible to mentally dismiss my surroundings and transpose my soul to another place and another time. To Rock Creek Park on a Sunday afternoon with the smell of the ground close to you and the faint sound of the creek trickling in your ear, children running around playing, laughing and screaming.

"Can I sit down beside you?"

My dream was broken. I opened my eyes and shielded them from the sun. From my prone position, I was looking at the biggest man I had ever seen.

"Sit anywhere you want to, buddy."

He did. Right next to me with his hand on my leg. I sat up quickly.

"Take it easy, honey. I ain't gonna eat you, yet!" He laughed and rolled back on the grass. "What's your name?"

"Eddie."

"You just come in today?"

"Yeah."

My eyes were beginning to focus. This wasn't a man at all. He had on make-up, heavy powder, lipstick, and even a skirt.

"What's your name?"

"Spivey."

"What the fuck do you want from me?"

I didn't have any interest in him at all and I wished the hell he would leave me alone.

"Want a cigarette?"

"No, I don't want a cigarette!"

I went back over to the basketball court without looking back at Spivey, but I could hear him kissing at me.

I now became more aware of the people around me. I spotted at least ten sissies who were very obvious. One thing I was also aware of: I was comparing everything to the jail. I had lost my awareness of the streets. At the jail the sissies could not walk around freely, nor could they dress the way they did here. I guess the difference was in the institutions. The hospital saw them as patients to be treated; the jail saw them as animals to be put in cages.

Recreation was soon over and we went inside. Spivey waved to me as I was going in but I pretended not to see him.

My first night at St. E.'s was frightening. Just before bedtime, a line formed at the nurse's office for medication. I found out that most of the patients were taking thorazine, a strong tranquillizer, which accounted for the zombie-like trance. Some of them got very violent if they were either not given their medicine or not given enough of it. I sat up in bed pretending to read a book until the lights were turned out. I had moved a trash can close to my bed to use for a weapon if I needed it and untucked the sheets so that I could get out of the bed in a hurry. I drifted off to sleep in a couple of hours. I was halfway when I noticed the sound of someone walking around. I opened my eyes just enough to see through my eyelashes. There was almost total quiet in the dormitory except for my own breathing.

The body was on the other side of the dormitory, hiding behind a post. It slid down the post to its hands and knees and wiggled on its belly across the lighted portion of the dorm. Now it was on my side; I couldn't tell exactly where it was or which direction it was moving in. I only knew that I was scared as hell and if it came up beside my bed I'd try to kill it.

Its hand came up three beds away and touched the lump that appeared to be asleep. The lump moved. Slowly it pushed the covers aside and disappeared between the beds. The muted sounds of lovemaking were faintly audible in the darkness.

The following day was full of activity for me. After breakfast, I talked to my doctor and had to explain to him that I didn't want to have sex with my mother, nor did I hate my father. I was put through a battery of psychological tests and asked all kinds of silly questions. I was also permitted to put Maxine on my visiting list.

Orson White was transferred to the hospital that morning. There was plenty to talk to him about. I gave him a tour and told him what Sullivan had told me and more that I had found out for myself. Around lunchtime, L. A. Harris visited us. He had talked to Stanley Stevenson, a key government witness, and found out that the government had threatened to put him in jail if he didn't testify against us. Stanley was also going to tell that to the court.

L. A. didn't stay very long. "You guys just relax and enjoy yourselves while you can. Ninety days can go pretty damn fast. If you find out anything else, be sure to contact me."

After lunch we went outside for recreation. Orson's reaction to the recreation yard was the same as mine. I saw Spivey lying on the grass, near the wall. It looked like he was waiting for someone, like a spider waiting for the fly—blanket spread on the grass, radio, cookies, and an icy container of Kool-Aid.

We passed him at least three times and I pretended not to notice as we approached him the fourth time.

"Hi, Eddie. Who's your friend?"

"You'd better stop fuckin' with me, man, before you get hurt. I don't like faggots and that means you."

"What's his story?" Orson asked.

"I don't know, man. I was playing ball yesterday and he tried to put the make on me."

"You should have hit him in his head with something!"

"I will if he keeps pressing me."

I would have—not because I felt threatened but because it would give me a reputation for not "fooling around," and it's absolutely necessary to have a reputation in order to live in jail. I knew of young boys who had reputations for being afraid to fight, and they were bullied into all kinds of situations. Older, bigger inmates took their commissary items and eventually their manhood. The stories that you hear about young boys' being sexually molested in prison are true. Only the strong survive, and in prison the strong are often confused with the insane.

It's difficult to determine when you might be in a situation that requires you to prove your manhood, but you always have to be prepared for it.

Orson knew one of the attendants, and we stopped to talk to him.

"What do you have to do as an attendant?" Orson asked.

"I don't do a damn thing, man. I just be here, that's all. We are supposed to keep you guys calm and make reports to the doctor on your behavior. A lot of guys come over here and play crazy so they can beat their charges. We are suppose to rap to you, play ball with you, and try to find out if you're jiving or not. There is some weird shit going on here, man. Whenever we have recreation the doctors spy on everybody from the windows and make notes.

"It's hard as hell to play crazy and get away with it. You're being observed all the time. A lot of guys play crazy when they talk to the doctor and they act normal the rest of the time.

"It's some crazy motherfuckers in here though. They just locked Carlton Smith up for hitting a guy in the head for talking to his woman."

"To his woman?"

"Yeah, Spivey! You've probably seen a big, tall, white faggot who always wears short shorts or skirts."

"Yeah, we've seen him!"

"Well, that's the one."

Spivey was still lying over by the wall and watching us. Recreation was ending and we went inside.

Orson was moved from Ward 5 that evening. Sullivan told me that the D.A.'s office had requested that we be kept separate, and they were moving Orson to another ward.

Was there anyplace that the government couldn't influence? There was no way that they could completely separate us, so why in the hell were they going through the motions?

It was on a Tuesday, after lunch, that I was informed I had a visitor. I was taken to the visiting room: Maxine was sitting there with my son. The visiting room was small and intimate. I went to the table where she was seated and kissed her.

"Hi. How you been?" she said.

I was so glad to see her I couldn't answer her questions. I merely sat down and held her hand. My son Reggy had gotten big. He was a little over a year old and vocal as hell. He started to cry and it was great to hear his voice. I played with him for a while and only a few words were spoken between Maxine and me. I didn't really know what to say to her. What the hell do you say to a young mother whose life should be just beginning but could very well be ending? I was glad she had brought Reggy. I could hide behind him for a while.

"I tried to come to see you, but they wouldn't let me."

"Yeah, I know."

"Reggy is big, isn't he?"

"Yeah."

"How long do you think it will be before they let you out?"

"Oh, it won't be very long. I'll be here for ninety days and then I'll go back to court. They'll probably let me out then."

"You really think so?"

"Yeah."

Then we started to talk. We talked about everything and everybody. It was so easy to make small conversation and pretend that things were different. She expected to go into the hospital in a couple of months. We talked about a possible name for the new baby, assuming that it would be a boy. The visit seemed to be over very quickly. I gave her hurried last-minute instructions: keep in touch with my lawyer; take care of herself and the baby; write to me as soon as she got home. There seemed to be so much to talk about and so many things for her to do for me. I was very sorry to see her leave. She looked kind of funny and walked like most pregnant women do in their seventh month. I felt very warm toward her in that instant. I had missed her very much.

There were more bouts with the doctor the following day. He wanted to know all about my childhood and school days. He wanted to know when I first masturbated, not *if* I had masturbated as a child, but "when I first started"! This doctor was weird. He had a thick funny mustache, heavy black horn-rimmed glasses, and an odd-shaped pointed head. I could just imagine him with a pair of binoculars peeping out the window at the patients in the yard.

Even though I had been instructed not to talk to anyone about the case, I did talk to Lawyer Williams. He wasn't just a jailhouse lawyer. He had been a colleague of my attorney, Perry W. Howard. Lawyer Williams was a fascinating person. He wrote motions and petitions for a lot of the patients and some were released. I never asked him anything about his case and I honestly don't think he remembered anything about it anyway—a mental block is what the doctors called it.

He had no mental block about the law, though; we spent hours going over the legal aspects of my case. He told me how the police had violated the *Federal Rules of Criminal Procedure* in my case and that there were grounds for dismissal of the charge. He also said that the false confessions should not be admitted into evidence, and if they were I should file a motion for immediate dismissal. He also said that we should not permit ourselves to be tried collectively;

we should demand separate trials. There was no way for us to be found guilty if we were tried separately. I made sure that I understood everything he said and made notes. He also gave me law books and court opinions to read. I kept myself very busy studying the D.C. Code and recent opinions from the Appeals Court. I was only interested in murder cases and soon learned a great deal.

I was able to talk to my mother and Maxine about the legal aspects of the case now, and even though they didn't understand what the hell I was talking about, I appeared to be very confident that we were going to win the case, and that was enough for them. It was hard for me to accept some of the things I read in the law books. It seemed to be just a bunch of meaningless words. For instance, from the time that Stanley's door was kicked in up until now, there had been a total disregard for the law. And in all the law that I had read, there was no mention that the police were exempt from obeying the law, but somehow I don't think anybody had ever told them! I concentrated on learning the law.

"Can I sit down with you?" I was lying in the yard when Spivey came over. He didn't wait for an answer. He had his goodies with him. "I read about you in the paper this morning." He handed me the paper.

It was a short article. L. A. Harris had filed a motion for a bill of particulars and had had a run-in with Frederick Smithson, the D.A. assigned to our case.

"I didn't know you were the one the papers were talking about."

"Yeah, I'm the one."

I wanted to find out more about what a bill of particulars was, so I went to look for Lawyer Williams.

The Fourth of July celebration at St. Elizabeth's was very freaky. We had a cookout in the yard. Several community groups came in and organized games, prepared food, and mingled with the nuts.

It was a hot day, very bright and festive. I had won a medal in one of the races and was walking around cooling off. There were a lot of women in the yard and it actually seemed like a picnic.

The homosexuals were competing with the women for the attention of their men. The women were arrayed in their sexiest miniskirts and some of them really looked good.

I ended up in my favorite spot next to the wall and was shortly joined by Spivey. Some other patients were coming out of the building. They had decided to let the locked ward out for the picnic. It was probably force of habit for the men to just start walking around the yard. Two of them stopped in front of us.

"What are you doing lying out here with this nigger?"

"We were just talking, honey."

"Just talking, huh?"

This must have been Carlton Smith, the guy who was locked up for hitting a guy in the head for talking to Spivey. I didn't move or say anything. He walked away, toward the recreation shack where the equipment was stored.

"What's wrong with him?"

"Oh, he's jealous as hell, that's all!"

Carlton Smith was coming back, but it was a little different this time. He had a baseball bat clutched tightly in his hand. He was followed by several of my friends who knew him well enough to know that he'd use the bat on somebody. As he approached, Spivey said, "You'd better leave. He'll kill you."

Leave! Where in the hell was I going to go? I wanted to leave, to get up and run. That would have been the sensible thing to do, but hell this wasn't a sensible situation. If I ran, my manhood would be running with me. Everybody was watching and I couldn't show that I was afraid. I'd have to face him, baseball bat and all.

"Get up, bitch, I'm gonna kick your ass!" he said to Spivey.

"I wasn't doing nothing, Smitty."

"I said to get up, damn it!"

Smitty hadn't paid me any attention at all. I started to move, and he turned. "You'd better stay where you are, Harrison, I ain't got no beef with you!"

Did I hear him right? He was copping out to me!

Carlton Smith was big, at least 6 feet, 3 inches, 250 pounds and with the bat he probably weighed 300 pounds, yet he was copping out to me, a measly little 140 pounds. I probably had a little extra weight, too, with all my friends standing around, and I took advantage of it.

"What you mean you ain't got no beef with me, sucker? You come running over here with a motherfuckin' bat threatening me like you got a beef."

"I'm not threatening you, man, I came over here to get my woman."

I decided not to press him any further or put him in a position where he'd have to use that bat, but I had to have one more word!

"Look, man, I ain't interested in your faggot, and I got enough trouble with one murder charge, so don't be fucking with me!"

"Come on, bitch!"

He grabbed Spivey by the arm and pulled him away. I purposely stayed out of his way for the remainder of the day. It wasn't easy to act tough, especially since I was scared to death.

I was beginning to feel very comfortable at St. E.'s, almost at home. Maxine or my mother visited me twice a week and I had enough law to keep me busy in the evenings. I had taught Sullivan how to play chess and I'd beat him two or three games a day for recreation.

After my visits with Maxine she would stand on a little bridge that led into the woods where I could watch her from my window. I would watch her for a long time and think of all the trouble she was having and was going to have. It was painful to watch her standing there. I always got the same impressions when I rushed to my window and saw her. How very much alone she was and how much she needed me. She visited me right up to the last moment of her pregnancy. One Tuesday my mother visited me and brought Reggy with her. She told me that Maxine had gone to the hospital and given birth to a boy that day. "We named him Eddie McArthur Harrison, Jr."

I was very happy but it didn't show at all. I was thinking that soon I would be going back to the jail and I probably wouldn't see her anymore, or my son. I played with Reggy and held him tightly. I felt that I could somehow love Reggy enough for both of them.

I was called for a visitor on Thursday, which was the day that Maxine usually came. I thought it was my mother but it wasn't. Maxine!

"What the hell are you doing here? Ain't you suppose to be home in bed?" I tried to be angry but I was happy as hell. I held her tightly, perhaps too tight.

"Take it easy, man. What are you trying to do, finish killing me?"

I released her so she could sit down. She looked good without the big stomach and umbrella dresses on.

"Would you tell me what you're doing here?"

She had a very simple and straightforward answer that made me almost melt with love for her!

"Because today is Thursday and I always visit you on Thursday, no matter what happens!"

She was obviously weak and tired from the walk from the bus stop, but she was very excited about the baby, I was very much aware of her dedication to me and I think at that moment more than any other time. I wanted to be free. My freedom would be decided in a court of law and I was anxious to have that decision. I was ready to face my accusers and tell what had happened.

IV

Back to Spoons

(Eddie)

On the day I was being transferred back to the jail, it seemed odd that the only one single thing I associated it with was "going back to spoons."

It was difficult to adjust during those first few weeks. It was like being a new man all over again. This time I was put on the first tier in Cell Block 2. This tier was divided into two parts—the detail men were on the first half and general population on the second half.

I was having trouble with the classification people because they wouldn't put Maxine on my visiting list. But it was easy to get letters to her. Everybody raised in the ghetto learns how to play con games for one reason or another—mostly because it's necessary to survive, because you have no choice. I was different only in the sense that I knew how to play it to perfection. Con never changes, only the stakes. In this instance I just wanted to get a letter to my woman.

Even white people understand con, but they don't use

it for the same purpose or call it the same thing. To the black street hustler it's con. To the white professional it's psychology! To both of them, if it's used properly, it gets you what you want!

Some of the guards were easy marks. Others were too stupid to be receptive. You can't play con on a guy if he doesn't have larceny in his heart. Being on the first tier, I was in closer contact with the guards and got to know a lot about them. I also learned very quickly that they would do favors for certain guys. I also saw how the tough guys were treated. I was learning how to "jail," to "do time."

You could have your cake and eat it too if you knew how to do time. Knowing how to do time was not "Jeffing" or "Uncle Tomming" at all but playing con. The only way to play con is to let the person you're playing *on* think they are playing on *you*. I got a job working in the dining room, cleaning tables and scrubbing floors three times a day. I had a little more freedom than before. I could even go to the other side of the cell block.

There was only one thing different about the two sides of Cell Block 2. One side was regular cell blocks; the other was Death Row. There were two guys on Death Row: Willie Jones and Willie Steward. It was officially called the "Administrative Segregation Range" or A.S.R. A few years earlier, the electric chair had been in the dining room on my side. I often looked at the cement floor where the chair had been bolted down and wondered how many men had died in that very spot. I heard stories about the smell of charred flesh lingering in the cell block for days after an execution.

I was always eager to run errands for the guards to save them a few trips up the steps, delivering newspapers, mail, or money receipts. Some of the guards were so lazy they would have gladly given you the keys to let guys out of the cells if they were not afraid they'd get caught.

The approach of my trial date brought mixed emotions: anxiety, fear, gladness. We had carefully gone over every little detail and we knew exactly what to expect. The D.A. assigned to our case represented the best they had to offer. Frederick Smithson was a professional prosecutor and a worthy adversary for L. A. Harris. These would be the main characters; one of them would win and the other would lose. First-degree murder carried a mandatory death sentence if Smithson won, and the odds were in his favor.

Smithson represented the United States of America and he commanded all its power and resources—the most powerful country in the world, feared because of its power, hated because of its power, admired because of its power.

The United States of America had been victorious in the War of 1812 just as it had been victorious in the Mexican-American War and in World War I and World War II against the Germans; and now the might and power of the United States of America was directed against Eddie M. Harrison.

"All rise. Hear ye, hear ye, hear ye. This honorable court is now in session. All persons having business before this court will be seated and come to order."

The bailiff's call never changed. It was the official signal that the fight had begun.

Judge Bernita Shelton Matthews was the only female judge in the District Court. She had a reputation for being fair and lenient. She was known as a sympathetic judge, easy on defendants. I thought we were lucky to have her for our trial.

The courtroom was filled to capacity.

"Members of the jury!" Judge Matthews spoke in a low-pitched but piercing tone aided by a concealed P.A. system. "The case to be tried in this courtroom is a case of first-degree murder. If convicted, the defendants will be sentenced to die in the electric chair. If you have any religious or moral scruples which will not permit you to sit on a case involving the death penalty, you may return to the jury room. Please give your name and reason for feeling that you cannot serve on this jury."

Several of the jurors stood and gave their names one at a time. They all had religious reasons contrary to the imposition of the death sentence and were dismissed. It would have been nice to have had all of them on the jury. The mere mention of the possibility of dying in the electric chair caused a cold chill to pass over me.

The prospective jurors were all seated in the back of the courtroom. There were approximately 150 of them, all shapes, colors, and sizes. Twelve of them would be selected to determine our guilt or innocence and whether we lived or died. There was no fence to straddle: life or death hung in the balance and it would be decided by twelve complete strangers, men and women whom I had never seen before and would probably never see again.

The judge continued: "The defendants in this case are Eddie M. Harrison, Orson G. White, and Joseph R. Sampson. Will the defendants please stand. Any jurors who are acquainted with any of the defendants, members of the defendants' families, or the deceased, George H. Brown, may be excused."

A few more of the jurors left the courtroom.

"The prosecutor in this case is Mr. Frederick Smithson." Smithson stood up and turned to face the jurors.

Judge Matthews then announced the names of the defense attorneys and stated that any members of the jury who were personally acquainted with any of these gentlemen would be excused. She continued to exclude members of the jury for various reasons. This whole process was designed to ensure that we would receive the benefit of a fair and impartial trial by a jury of our peers, without prejudice of any sort.

After the judge queried the jurors and the basic questions were asked, it was time to call the individual jurors to the jury box. In a capital case, the government is required to furnish defense counsel with a list of all prospective jurors, with their name, occupation, address, and age. L. A. Harris had gone over the list with us and we had a general idea of who we wanted on the jury. We had definite ideas of trying to get younger, inner-city, blue-collar workers, but Smithson would have none of that. The defense and the government could strike any member of the jury without giving reasons.

The jurors were called by name and asked to take a seat in the jury box. The first juror was a man so old that he was barely able to walk and he was hardly in his seat when L. A. Harris had him dismissed. The strategy for picking a jury is very involved. The professional workers are not so bad, or people who have the ability to analyze, scientists who know how to weigh facts, or even mechanics who deal with tangibles or people who do not work for the government and whose jobs might therefore not be at stake. The government workers are especially dangerous because of inter-agency reaction and the desire to cooperate with each other. We tried to exclude all government workers except the young black post office workers, whose attitude might be in our favor. Perry Howard seemed content to let L.A. Harris handle the selection of the jury. He merely sat there looking interested in what was happening. L. A. Harris was very serious about selecting the jury. His questions were hard and direct.

"Do any of you feel that simply because these boys are charged with this crime they are in fact guilty?"

"Do any of you feel that simply because a policeman testifies he is telling the truth?"

"Do you believe that a policeman would lie under oath?"

"I object, Your Honor!"

"Do any of you have members of your family on the police force?"

"Is there any reason why you cannot judge this case on the evidence presented in this courtroom?"

More and more questions were put to the jury and twelve jurors were finally selected, plus two alternates. There has been more than one case where jurors have disappeared and mistrials were declared.

Judge Matthews permitted the defense and prosecution to address opening remarks to the jury.

Smithson: "Ladies and gentlemen of the jury, the government will prove to you through the testimony of witnesses and evidence that on or about March 8, 1960, the three defendants went to the home of George H. Brown after following him from a restaurant and attempted to rob him; during the course of this attempted robbery, Eddie Harrison, the defendant sitting there in the brown suit, shot and killed George Brown. The government will prove its case to you so that you will have no reasonable doubt as to the guilt of Eddie M. Harrison, Joseph R. Sampson, and Orson G. White, and I will request that after careful deliberation of all the facts you bring back a verdict of guilty. It will not be easy for you. A guilty verdict carries with it a mandatory sentence of death by electrocution, but it is your duty to judge these men regardless of the penalty. Thank you."

"Mr. Harris?"

"I will reserve my comments, Your Honor."

"The court will call a recess until tomorrow morning, at which time you may proceed to call your first witness, Mr. Smithson.

"All rise. This honorable court stands recessed until nine o'clock tomorrow morning."

The trial lasted four weeks and it should have been billed as the best show in town—a complete mockery of everything that justice and the judicial system are supposed to represent. All of the witnesses from the inquest were called again and they repeated the same beautiful lies as before.

One startling difference in this trial was the availability

of two eyewitnesses: Olina McCoy, a lady who lived across the street from Cider George, and a man who said he was standing outside of Cider George's house shoveling coal as we ran out of the doorway.

The McCoy lady told the truth but the other man appeared from nowhere. Smithson and L. A. Harris were having a ball. It was a contest filled with courtroom antics that only a lawyer could appreciate. There were times when some of the jurors fell asleep from boredom and times when everyone in the courtroom, including the judge, was caught up in the excitement of what was happening.

On and on the prosecution witnesses came until it appeared that there would be no end of them. I had never seen most of them, but they were my accusers and they were doing their damndest to see that I died in the electric chair.

I sat quietly most of the time and watched. There wasn't a damn thing I could do. I couldn't even question the witnesses against me: just sit there and listen to the lies and absorb the staring eyes of the jurors. I was surprised to see the policeman who had almost killed me walk through the door and take the witness stand—the very same bastard that had kicked me in the chest at the police station.

"Do you swear to tell the whole truth and nothing but the truth so help you God?"

"I do."

"Will you state your name and occupation for the record, please."

"Sergeant ——, Metropolitan Police Department, Robbery Squad."

"Do you know any of the defendants seated at that table?"

"Yes, sir, I do!"

"Would you identify the defendant and tell this court and the jury how you came to know him, please."

"The gentleman sitting at the defense table in the brown suit and striped tie."

"Will the record show that the witness has identified the defendant Harrison?"

"It shall so reflect."

"The defendant Harrison, along with Orson White, Joseph Sampson, and Stanley Stevenson, was arrested on March 10 and taken to the Robbery Division for questioning in connection with the death of George Brown. He stated that he knew nothing of the circumstances surrounding the death of George Brown and after further questioning he was released."

While he was testifying, I got L. A.'s attention to let him know that this man was the one who had beaten me at the police station. I could barely sit still.

"Does defense counsel have any questions of this witness?"
"Yes, Your Honor!"
L. A. Harris: "Did you at any time while this boy was in custody beat or kick him?"
Witness: "Sir?"
Smithson: "Your honor, I object to the use of the term 'boy' being used by defense counsel."
Judge: "Objection sustained."
L. A. Harris: "Did you at any time hit, strike, kick, or otherwise inflict violence on Eddie Harrison while he was in custody?"
Witness: "Of course not!"
L. A. Harris: "Mr. ____, how long have you been a member of the Police Department?"
Witness: "Eight years, sir."

L. A. Harris's tone of voice had changed. He was talking very slowly, and he was being very kind to the witness. Something was up!

L. A. Harris: "Eight years you say?"
Witness: "Yes, sir!"
L. A. Harris: "Do you like working for the Police Department?"
Witness: "Yes, sir."
L. A. Harris: "Do you earn enough money to support yourself and your family by working?"
Smithson: "I object, Your Honor. Defense counsel is asking questions not related to direct examination."
Judge: "Objection sustained!"
L. A. Harris: "I'll withdraw the question, Your Honor. Sergeant____, have you ever been reprimanded for inflicting brutality on a suspect?"
Witness: "No, sir."
L. A. Harris: "Sergeant ____, didn't you in fact beat Eddie Harrison

for three hours in the police station when he refused to say what you wanted him to say?"

Witness: "No, sir."

L. A. Harris: "Sergeant ____, what would happen to a policeman who admitted to beating a suspect?"

Witness: "He would probably be dismissed from the force."

L. A. Harris: "Then I ask you, sir, if you had beaten Eddie Harrison, would you come into the courtroom and admit it? Will you answer the question, sir!"

The witness looked to Smithson for help. He had been set up and there was no answer.

SILENCE.

All of the jurors were looking at him and waiting for an answer that he couldn't give.

L. A. Harris waited for the exact psychological moment when the answer would be apparent to everyone! "I have no further questions, Your Honor. The answer is obvious!"

It felt good to see that policeman squirm, and be made to look like the bastard that he was.

The government's case went well. All of the witnesses testified as they were expected to. Thomas Leon "Hot Dog Tom" Young made a positive identification of Sampson as being seen in Key's restaurant as Brown and Young counted money on the table. Benjamin Eugene Valentine testified that I had admitted killing Brown. His testimony caused quite a bit of excitement. Judge Matthews interrupted Smithson to ask if I had mentioned the reason for going to Brown's house the day before the murder. The answer to that question was the most important piece of evidence in the entire trial.

The basis for the government's case was that Cider George was killed during an attempted robbery and the burden of proof was entirely theirs. Since Cider had over $2,000 in his pocket when the police arrived, the government was hard pressed to prove that a robbery had taken place. They had to establish that there was an attempt to commit robbery, which means they had to prove my "intentions." Absolutely no one in the courtroom knew my intentions except me, and I had been advised not to take the stand to testify in my behalf.

"No, he didn't say why he went there. Someone came into the restaurant and we stopped talking." Smithson didn't seem pleased with his answer. He had obviously expected him to say something different. However, Smithson didn't lean on him too heavily. Valentine was a very shaky witness, extremely nervous and scared. He couldn't face me when he walked into court. He obviously felt that he was betraying friendship and he couldn't bear to look me in the eye.

Under cross-examination, L. A. Harris tore Valentine to pieces. I felt sorry for him. He had gotten involved in this case by pure accident and he was paying a heavy price. He was visibly torn between his fear of the U.S. Attorney, his commitment to our friendship, and the community he would have to return to as the guy who "told" on Eddie. Eugene was as much the victim of circumstance as I was, and the price he would pay would be great.

Smithson's second surprise was the testimony of Stanley Stevenson. Stanley was expected to testify in behalf of the government, but it didn't quite turn out that way. He said that he didn't know anything at all about the case and was only testifying because Smithson had threatened to charge him with being an accomplice if he didn't testify against us. He was charging Smithson with coercing a witness into giving false testimony! A very serious charge that could have gotten Smithson disbarred, fired, and possibly sent to jail if proven! But it didn't turn out that way either. Smithson was a representative of the United States of America. Shortly after Stanley's "testimony" he was "arrested for possession of narcotics" and sent to prison for twelve years. "Shortly after" might be misleading. It was immediately after.

The best show in town was a sellout each day, always filled to capacity. All of the newspapers were represented and gave a daily account of the progress of the trial. The newspaper accounts were much more exciting than the actual trial. If a witness didn't show up to testify, the following day's headline would read "Key Witness Disappears in Cider George Murder Case"; or when the government played tricks for the jurors that didn't work, the papers picked it up right away. On one occasion, Smithson had one of his assistants bring two empty, sealed boxes into the courtroom and place them on the table in front of the jurors. L. A. Harris objected to the boxes being in the courtroom and asked to have them removed. The following day's newspaper read "Two Boxes of Evidence Dismissed from Cider George Murder Case." The jury only saw the boxes of "evidence." They didn't get the benefit of knowing they were empty.

Near the conclusion of the government's case, we began to develop our defense. It was very simple. The legal prerequisites had not been satisfied to sustain a felony murder conviction. It was either first-degree murder or no form of murder. The important facts were not that Cider George had been killed or that I had killed him. The all-important factor was *how* he was killed. The government had to prove that it happened during an attempted robbery and that proof must be substantiated by independent evidence, of which there was none! Our defense rested on a pure legal question and the entire scope of the trial changed. I was no longer on trial for murder. The judicial system was on trial for justice. How I prayed that we would both win. How I looked forward to justice being done. How I looked forward. . . .

The government's case was good and if we relied on the jury to decide guilt or innocence based on the evidence presented in the court, we'd surely lose.

The legal issue was not our only defense; that was a matter for the judge to decide. We also had a jury to contend with. I demanded to take the stand and testify, to explain, to give some account of what had really happened, to plead and try to make the jurors understand why I had not gone to the police in the beginning, why I had not explained to them what had happened.

L. A. Harris didn't want me to take the stand, but I could not sit there and be accused of murder and not deny it. I couldn't sit there and by my silence make it easy for them to send me to the electric chair.

So I did take the stand. I tried to answer the questions as best I could. I spoke in a low voice and could not hide my fear and anxiety. I was a bad witness but I told the truth and it seemed to me that that was all that was necessary—to tell the truth!

The jurors were perched on the edges of their chairs and seemed to absorb my every word. Their piercing stares seemed to go through me, into me, probing, searching.

I testified for approximately four hours. The cross-examination by Smithson was very intense. He tried to tear me apart, to make it appear that I was lying to save my neck. His insinuations were harsh, cruel, and totally unsympathetic. Smithson was a professional prosecutor and I, just a scared boy. It was difficult not to hate him, not to vent my frustrations and hate on him as an individual.

After four weeks of trial, both sides rested their cases and L. A. Harris filed a motion for a Directed Verdict of Acquittal based on the government's not having proved its case. There was absolutely no independent evidence to support a felony murder conviction. He made a very strong case and I was very hopeful that the motion would be granted.

The motion was denied. It was our only real chance, but L. A. Harris was good with juries, too. He made a very dramatic presentation to the jury, a fiery speech that was at times soft and hypnotic. He pleaded for a verdict of not guilty and told them that it was their duty to find me not guilty if there was a shadow of doubt about my guilt. Just before this argument was completed, he collapsed in front of the jury box. Those who were not moved to tears during his oration were reached with his final dramatic move. The arguments were adjourned as L. A. was removed to the hospital. The doctor reported to the court the following morning that he had suffered an attack caused by complete exhaustion and needed a few days' rest.

After L. A. came out of the hospital, the case went to the jury for deliberation, and after two and a half days the jury reached its verdict.

We were told to stand and face the jury.

"Mr. Foreman, has the jury reached a verdict?"

"Yes, Your Honor."

"How do you find the defendants?"

"We find the defendants, Eddie M. Harrison, Joseph R. Sampson, and Orson G. White, guilty of murder in the first degree."

All hell broke loose in the courtroom; reporters rushed into the hallways. The marshals seemed to get edgy and move closer to us. L. A. had the jury polled and each juror in turn uttered a single word, "Guilty!"

I felt pain in my jaw and realized that I had been clenching my teeth and holding my breath.

The jury was quickly dismissed and we were returned to jail to await sentencing.

Three months after the verdict I was still very much in shock. I often went to the other side of the cell block and looked at the death cells, wondering which one would be mine. I also tried to prepare my family for the day when I would go to court for sentencing. Unlike most prisoners, I didn't have to suffer each night, wondering how much time I would get. What was the sense of that? I knew I was going to get all that the law allowed.

It was approximately seven months before I was sentenced. It also seemed to be the beginning of the end of the world. Just prior to sentencing, I was informed that Perry W. Howard had died of a heart attack and the court was going to appoint a new attorney to represent me. My mother had gone into considerable debt to retain Perry W. Howard, and I felt cheated of something when he died. Hell, he didn't have a right to die yet. It was very bad timing. Judge Matthews officially appointed L. A. Harris to represent me at sentencing.

V

May God Have Mercy on Your Soul

(Eddie)

"Does the defendant have anything to say before sentence is passed?"

"No!"

"Eddie M. Harrison, you have been found guilty upon an indictment charging the offense of Murder in the First Degree while Attempting to Perpetrate the Crime of Robbery, and, upon the verdict of guilty you are hereby sentenced to the punishment of death by electrocution, and it is

"ORDERED, that you, Eddie M. Harrison, be forthwith taken to the District of Columbia Jail, otherwise known as the Washington Asylum and Jail, in the District of Columbia, and there be kept in close confinement; and that on the 21st day of July, 1961, you be taken to the place prepared for your execution in the District of Columbia Jail, and that then and there you be electrocuted according to law; AND MAY GOD HAVE MERCY ON YOUR SOUL!"

VI

The Wait for Death

(*Eddie*)

Death Row wasn't so bad after you got used to it. The effect of being there was kind of tranquilizing because there was absolutely nothing to do except be there. The death sentence was held in abeyance pending the outcome of appeal, which would take at least a year, so I wasn't actually worried about dying in the electric chair any time soon. As a matter of fact, I had no intention of dying in the electric chair at any time. At twenty years of age, I hadn't begun to live yet and it was certainly no time to consider dying.

I went through a lot of changes while on Death Row. There was a lot of time to go through changes. Reflections on how I had come to be there caused me to be extremely bitter against the courts and police. I was very anti-establishment, which means I was extremely anti-white. It was easy to blame Whitey for all the bad things that happened to me. I was arrested by a white man, prosecuted by a white man, sentenced to die by a white woman, and the sentence was to be carried out by a white man. It was indeed easy to hate Whitey, to loathe Whitey, and to rebel against Whitey and all that he stood for.

I came across a lot of the Black Muslim literature and began to study it intensely. I was fascinated by some of the things I learned about myself as a black man and even more so by what I learned about the white man. I had never known very much about the history of the black man. Most of the history I studied in school concerned the white man, the United States, and colored people. The Muslim literature traced the history of the black man back to the beginning of time when there was no white race. It even gave an account of the creation of the white race, where it was created, why it was created, and who created it!

It was strange that I should have found an outlet for my hostility in a religious movement. I changed quite a bit in the few months that followed the imposition of the death sentence. I discovered that I had been dead for the last 400 years that my people were in bondage. I discovered that I had been robbed, raped, and put to death on the day of conception in my mother's womb. And now the filthy, dirty, pink-skin, blue-eyed devil wanted me to stop breathing! Well kiss my ass, Whitey, I refuse to die in your fuckin' electric chair! You've robbed me of my heritage, raped me of my manhood, and you are a goddamn fool because you let me find out about it. I became so engrossed in the study of Islam, I completely forgot about the death sentence. I completely forgot about myself because there was no self. My entire being was the product of a white racist society beginning with my very name! I set about the business of finding out just who the hell I was, of redefining values, morals, principles, and scruples. It was no easy task.

Orson had also become interested in Islam and we often studied the same material and helped each other with our lessons. There was never a period in my life when I was more obsessed with anything that faintly resembled a religion. But then, Islam was not really a religion by religious standards. Islam was a culture, a way of life, an ideology whose basic fundamentals were the belief in One God "Allah" and self-discipline. I didn't have any problems adjusting. It was just what I wanted and needed. I remembered Fulwood and how he had stood up against the guards and cursed them in front of all of the other inmates, openly rebelling against them without fear. Something had given him the courage to stand up against them, knowing what would happen but not being afraid to confront them.

I learned my lessons well and developed an intensive hate and distrust toward all white people and the white establishment which controlled everything. I read the so-called "Holy Bible" and was taught to interpret the Book of Revelations. The Muslims called it the "Poison Book" and it indeed caused the mental deceit of all those who read it and accepted it without understanding it. But at the same time it provided insight and knowledge to all who had the key to unlock its mystery and feed on the fruit of life. I also studied the Holy Koran, Torah, and all other writings of the holy prophets. My reading material also included the works of the major philosophers and sociologists, as well as recent court decisions. Out of all my studies, it developed that the most practical and necessary was the study of law.

After about four months of study, praying, and fasting, I began to realize that some very definite and positive changes had occurred in my attitude. My studies had broadened my perspective and made me painfully aware of the many social and economic injustices inflicted on me as a person and on my people. I felt as though I should share no blame or responsibility for the situation that I was in. I was a complete and total victim, a direct product of an environment and sub-culture that I could not escape—a deadly environment where every living moment is a last breath and a sub-culture that was created 400 years ago by the white slave traders for the purpose of making me believe that I was inferior.

Why should I be held responsible for my actions? A drunk is not responsible for his actions while under the influence of alcohol, nor a drug addict under the influence of drugs. Why then should a nigger be held responsible for his actions while under the influence of racism?

It's all your fault, Whitey. What the hell do you expect?

As my hate for white people continued to grow, my love, compassion, and concern for black people began to develop. I began to think of all black people as brothers and sisters. All black people could be excused for their behavior because they were not really themselves, but a personification of all the evil and hate of the white people that was learned when we were robbed of our own culture and heritage.

God, the bitterness and hate that I felt!

VII

Daniel Jackson Oliver Wendell Holmes Morgan a/k/a L. A. Harris

(Eddie)

I was lying on my bed one day reading and vaguely listening to the radio. I heard a news report that the police were searching for an ex-convict named Daniel Jackson Oliver Wendell Holmes Morgan, who was suspected of having posed as an attorney named L. A. Harris and who had represented three convicted Negro boys sentenced to die in the electric chair. Daniel Morgan, the radio announced, had been exposed as a fake by an attorney who had recognized him from a prior newspaper article.

I jumped from my bed and yelled to Orson.

"Brother Orson."

"Yes, sir?"

"Did you hear that?"

"Yes sir. I didn't catch it all, only the part about L. A. Harris representing three brothers under the death sentence. We'd better check it out!"

It didn't take long to check. The evening newspapers were full of stories about L. A. Harris and the fact that he had represented us. The following morning papers carried it even bigger. According to the stories, L. A. Harris had been involved in an automobile accident with a woman attorney who remembered having seen his picture in a magazine article. The lawyer couldn't remember exactly what the connection was, but it had something to do with him posing as an attorney. L. A. didn't wait around for her to figure it out. He panicked when she started to inquire and left town. The Police Department had issued a warrant for his arrest and were searching the city for him. The story of L. A. Harris caused quite a stir in the jail. We were not his only clients. L. A. Harris had also represented Emanuel Pea, who was on Death Row awaiting execution for killing his wife and attempting suicide. He had also represented several men charged with armed robbery, who were serving 5- to 15-year sentences.

For the first time I was somewhat shaken at the thought of being on Death Row. I felt alone and deserted. I had a tremendous amount of faith in L. A. Harris and trusted that he would get me out of this trouble. I was probably developing a real persecution complex. It seemed as though fate was really trying to fuck me around. Perry Howard's death was one thing: now I had the feeling that L. A. Harris was taken away from me. My very first feelings were of shock and anger at L. A. Harris. I thought he had crossed me! How in the hell could he not be a lawyer? You don't just walk into a courtroom and practice law without being a lawyer. The whole thing was ridiculous. Didn't the court know the lawyers who were licensed to practice before them? You damn sure had to be a member of the Bar!

L. A. Harris had to have a lot of nerve to take this case, knowing that our lives were at stake. I don't know why he did it, but one thing I do know, he sure didn't do it for money.

After the initial shock and anger were over, I was quite amused. It was amusing to know that a black man who had never been to law school could make a complete and total mockery of the whole judicial system by posing as an attorney and doing a much better job of defending the rights of people accused of crimes than the lawyers with degrees who had spent years in law school. Licensed or not, L. A. Harris was one hell of a lawyer and I hoped they'd never catch him. Run, Black Man, run!

L. A. Harris had already filed a "Notice of Appeal" in our case, so we were in the jurisdiction of the U.S. Court of Appeals. I was very encouraged because of my legal situation, as it turned out. It looked like L. A. Harris had won the case for me after all.

It happens to be illegal for the court to try a person for a capital offense without the defendant being represented by an attorney. Not only had I been illegally tried and convicted without the right to proper counsel, but also sentenced to die in the electric chair! Funny how things were developing; the aces in this game kept changing hands. The government had them but didn't know how to play the game. Now I held the aces and I was going to be damn sure to play them right.

L. A. Harris had been arrested, and was waiting to be extradited back to the District of Columbia, but still I sat on Death Row waiting for the court to take some action. They didn't really give a damn that my constitutional rights had been violated. They should have at least ordered a new trial, but they wanted to deny me even that. Well, I had news for them. The last thing in the world I wanted was a new trial. I wanted my freedom!

According to the Constitution of the United States, a person cannot be put in double jeopardy of life or limb. Since it was obvious that they could not just put me to death, there was only one other choice: to give me my goddamn freedom!

The question of double jeopardy was a legal one, and I went to great pains to preserve it. If I had requested a new trial and it were granted, I would be waiving my right to claim double jeopardy because I would have been the party to initiate the action that brought me to trial. But if the court or the government initiated the action, I could most certainly claim double jeopardy.

There was very little communication with the courts. We were careful not to send anything to the court that could be considered a motion for a new trial. I sat on Death Row waiting for something to break loose.

It would seem that the U.S. Department of Justice would have made some attempt to correct the injustice of three men convicted of murder and sentenced to die as soon as it was suspected that any constitutional rights were violated.

It would seem that the United States Court would have taken some corrective action. It would also seem that the United States Attorney's office would recognize that by arresting L. A. Harris they were also saying that we had been denied legal representation.

There were a number of things that could have been done in the interest of justice, but the only one concerned with justice was me! None of the people whose responsibility justice is was concerned about it. It was a shame that this was not the year when it was fashionable for the white establishment to give justice to black people.

There were times when uncertainty set in, when I doubted that I was doing the right thing. The other men on Death Row were doing everything in the world to get a new trial, to be relieved of the pressure of being confined in a cell for twenty-four hours, to be relieved of the possibility of dying, to be given another chance at freedom or a lesser sentence.

My family often advised me to take the opportunity, to stop "playing with death" and come to my senses, but I didn't feel that way. If I could endure the pressure when I was weak, I could damn sure stand it now that I was strong.

VIII

Just-us

(Eddie)

Nine months after I had been sentenced to death, the United States Court of Appeals decided to send the case back to the District Court to entertain a motion for a new trial.

This order of remand was a perfect example of the double standard of justice in America. The court was in a very embarrassing position because of L. A. Harris, and there was only one way for them to get out of it. They were tired of waiting for us to make a mistake and file a motion for a new trial. Now they were openly suggesting that we do so.

The order also said that we had ten days to file the motion. I also got a letter from the District Court saying they had received the order of the Appellate Court and had appointed a lawyer to represent me on the motion. I wrote a letter to the lawyer requesting that he visit me immediately. Five of the days had already passed and it would take two more days for him to get the letter.

The lawyer didn't show up at the jail, and on the tenth day I was called to a small room in the central lock-up of the courthouse.

The lawyer was a funny-looking man, short, fat, bald-headed, and white. I was sure that he had a license to practice law: he looked like it.

"Mr. Harrison, I was appointed by the court to represent you on this motion for a new trial."

I shook his hand and sat down across the table from him. I was just about to tell him that "we" were not going to file a motion for a new trial.

"I got your letter, but I figured that since I'd be seeing you today, there wasn't any reason for me to come all the way over to the jail. I filed the motion for a new trial this morning."

"You did *what?*" My ass hadn't gotten to the chair before I was on my feet again, raging with anger.

"You did *what?*" I couldn't believe it. All the time and agony spent preserving this precious chance at freedom thrown away by a total stranger because he didn't think it necessary to come all the way over to the jail! The lawyer looked perplexed and I guess he should have been. "You filed a motion for a new trial, huh? Well, I think you'd better take your ass up there and withdraw it right now!"

I explained all the circumstances to him, and after a while it began to dawn on him that he had fucked up!

We were called before Judge Matthews and the lawyer requested to have the motion withdrawn. Judge Matthews had been prepared to grant the motion, and the move to withdraw came as a shock to her. The order of the court was quite clear: the court had been instructed to "entertain a motion for a new trial" and could not move on any other issues.

Judge Matthews instructed me to stand before the court.

"Mr. Harrison, this action is before the court on remand from the U.S. Court of Appeals for the District of Columbia for the purpose of entertaining a motion for a new trial. I understand that your lawyer filed such a motion this morning and is now requesting to have it withdrawn?"

"Your Honor, he filed the motion without my knowledge or consent, and I requested him to withdraw the motion because I do not feel it is in my best interest!"

"Since the court does not have any authority beyond this action, the case is hereby remanded back to the U.S. Court of Appeals for further procedures."

I was returned to Death Row while they pondered what to do with my case.

Finally, the court reversed the case without a decision and remanded it to the District Court for trial. I had won, I was sure—it would be a clear-cut case of double jeopardy and I would have to be turned loose.

IX

Trial by Jury (Legal)

(*Eddie*)

The reversal by the Appeals Court attracted a lot of publicity, and as a result the case was becoming more and more famous. I received letters from newspaper reporters wanting statements and little old ladies telling me to thank "God" for being spared.

The court appointed George J. Thomas to represent me at trial. This was the lawyer I wanted to get in the beginning but was unable to. He was a well-respected trial lawyer who specialized in murder cases. I had read of a number of cases that he had won.

Although George felt that we had a very good case of double jeopardy, he made me aware of a much better point that would probably win my freedom: the denial of a speedy trial!

Since the court ruled that the first trial was illegal, it was in effect saying that I was denied my constitutional right to a speedy trial. I had been locked up for almost three years before receiving a "legal" trial!

George didn't have much hope that we would win the case on its merits, but the constitutional questions were another thing.

Law itself is strange. There are so many different courts, many often lorded over by a sick, senile white man who thinks he's God holding sheep accountable for eating grass from the wrong pasture. The courts across the land are autonomous and localized. The law of the land is also fucked up to the point where it's possible to prove anything at all with a number of legal opinions from judges to support just about any point at all!

I had a number of conversations with George Thomas during the period between the Appellate reversal and the second trial. We were building our defense around the constitutional questions and relying on the record to rebut the government's case.

I felt very confident having George as my attorney; he had a calmness about him that was somehow passed on to me. My confidence in him also enabled me to continue my studies. The daylight hours continued to move rapidly. There was always another book to read, letters to write, or shouted conversations up or down the tier.

Recreation on Death Row was simply a fifteen minute walk on the tier. Each man was let out of his cell separately and permitted to walk the tier—all seventy-five feet of it—up and down, up and down; if you hurried, you could get in as many as 150 laps. It's strange how being locked in such a small space broadens your perspective. I was able to see myself in relation to other things and spent a lot of time trying to figure out exactly where I fit into the total scheme of my reality. The jail . . . Death Row . . . society . . . human race . . . family . . . politics . . . religion.

Life is like a huge puzzle and each of us has a place where only we can fit. Some of us are big pieces, some little pieces, some square, some round, but all of us fit somewhere and all of us are attached to something else and related to the total picture. We devote our lives to answering one simple question: "Where in the hell do I fit?" I knew for sure that I didn't fit in a cell on Death Row, and I also knew for sure that I was a big piece of the puzzle of life, but the all-important question was still, "Where in the hell do I fit?"

Since only eight of the cells on Death Row were occupied, the other half of the tier was used as M.S.U. (Maximum Security Unit). The prisoners who couldn't adjust in general population or who were separated for their own protection were sent to M.S.U. There were also a few prisoners on M.S.U. who had serious mental problems. M.S.U. was the "catch all" unit for any situation that the administration couldn't deal with.

If you refused to eat leftover garbage from your tray, they would send you to M.S.U. (after you came out of the hole, where they would almost make you beg for that same garbage), or if you finally *demanded* to see a doctor after listening to lies all day long.

Not everyone can take M.S.U.; it's worse than Death Row. The only thing you are entitled to there is food! Showers, recreation, and visits are optional.

As things began to move, I once again got caught up in the excitement of preparing for trial. I knew every point of law that we were going to argue and all the cases we would use in support. L. A. Harris soon found his way back to the District of Columbia Jail. This time he was an inmate! The jail grapevine quickly spread the news of L. A.'s admission. I had even arranged to have him put in our cell block. I was unsure of how to react to him, but I knew that in the long run we were very fortunate to have had him representing us.

I don't think I'll every forget the first time I talked to him from Death Row. I was lying on my bed reading when I heard his voice from the dining room.

"Say, Eddie?"

I stood slowly and looked down into the dining room. "Hey L. A., how you doing?"

"Say listen, don't you worry about a thing. You have a free ticket right out of this place if you play your cards right!"

L. A. looked kind of scared at first; I guess he was as uneasy as I was. He didn't know how I felt about him and I know he was very tense. It was most certainly a strange encounter.

I imagine that clients before me have found themselves in jail with their attorneys, but hell, mine wasn't even an attorney! L. A. Harris dressed in unpressed blue jeans and a rumpled blue shirt was still very much the dynamic lawyer. We talked for a while about the status of the case, and he agreed that our double jeopardy point was a winner. It's even stranger how the lawyer/client relationship was still intact. Hell, I now knew that he didn't have a license to practice law, but who ever said that a license was the basis for one person to advise another. I still had a great deal of respect for L. A. Harris and I knew that he had represented me as well as any lawyer could have, probably even better than most!

I spent a lot of time talking to L. A. during the following months and learned much from him. We spent hours going over the testimony from the previous trial.

The second trial began on April 22, 1963, with the ritual of stacking the deck against the defense! A jury of my peers was selected, none of whom was under thirty years old or had any prior record. All of my peers were considered unfit for jury duty, but that's a minor constitutional guarantee reserved for white-collar criminals.

The peers selected for me were mostly middle-class white folks or would-be middle-class niggers who didn't think there was any difference.

Immediately after the jury was sworn in, the trial had legally begun. We raised our precious points and were literally shocked at the judge's response!

The judge listened to our arguments and the constitutional questions but refused to make a ruling! He stated that these questions were for the Court of Appeals to decide. He was saying that the only way for us to have these questions ruled on was to be convicted again and go to the Court of Appeals. The whole outcome of the trial was decided in that ten-minute argument. It was apparent that the judge's intentions were to have us convicted.

The damn fool, it was his *duty* to rule on those questions. It was literally a matter of life or death . . . MINE! George Thomas was apparently very upset also. We had counted heavily on these points. Orson and Sampson were also shocked. My talks with George before the trial paid off. I tried like hell not to show any reaction to the judge's decision. "Keep cool, Eddie, don't blow up. The jury will be watching you every minute. Look relaxed, take it easy." I fought to remain silent and in my seat when my senses drove me to scream!

We all knew that it was just a matter of time before it would be over. The only real question was whether we would be sentenced to life imprisonment or death! The trial no longer mattered. I mentally dismissed everything that was happening and began to prepare myself for the inevitable conviction. It was very easy to dismiss everything. I think most people learn how to do that at a very early age. Even the most important things can be dismissed if we choose not to face them.

Well, I chose not to face the fact that shortly this little man with the bald head and the black robe was going to tell me either that I was going to spend the rest of my life in jail or that I was going to die in the electric chair!

Quite a lot to dismiss, I will admit, but I did it! Actually the trial from that point on was very interesting. I became keenly aware of what was actually happening in the courtroom.

Instead of reacting as a participant, I became an observer, trying to figure out why people were playing the roles they were in. Hell, since in principle I knew the outcome, it was more fun to watch the conspiracy against me. I had mastered the art of self-control and it was easy to project myself out of the picture. Orson and Ray weren't as fortunate.

The court recessed for lunch and we were being escorted to the cell block. All of us were very depressed; the morning had not gone well at all.

"All right, move." I heard the command from one of the marshals.

"I'm moving goddamit!" responded Ray.

I was in front of Ray, and Orson was in the back.

"I said move!" yelled the marshal.

I turned around. Orson was shoved by the marshal, causing all of us to stumble into the lock-up cell. That was the straw that broke the camel's back! Orson turned on the marshal and pulled him into the cell. The two of them began to tussle on the floor. Two more marshals quickly moved into the cell and tried to subdue Orson. Ray tried to pull the marshals off Orson but his intentions went unnoticed.

Pretty soon there was a "free for all" brawl going on. I stood back and watched. It sounded like someone was being killed. The courtroom door burst open and more marshals streamed into the cell. It was over as quickly as it had started.

When the trial convened, Orson and Ray were returned to the courtroom in chains and handcuffs. The judge had been informed of the fracas and he had ordered them bound with chains. The trial continued and the jury was instructed to disregard the chains. It had nothing to do with the trial, they were told!

How in the hell could a jury not consider the fact that they were in chains. Who would tell them what really happened? I didn't have any part in it, but who in the hell cared?

This was my legal trial, three years after being convicted

illegally. The physical chains were not the only kinds. I was bound by a legal system that in no way would let me free. George Thomas even went through the motion of filing for a mistrial. Another waste of time. It didn't take long to convict us. This time the court didn't show any sympathy at all. We were all sentenced to life imprisonment—a punishment harsher than death.

Now what!

The only guarantee of ever being released from prison was the eventuality of death. I found an alternative to this problem in reading and studying. In death only my body would leave these walls and in life only my body would be contained.

Freedom is not a matter of one's ability to move from place to place, but the unrestricted movement of one's thoughts and his state of mind. How many "slaves" willingly leaped to their death as the slave-trader crossed the Atlantic? How many "free" men shared the profits of that human cargo? Freedom cannot be defined in terms of space and, as little of it as I had, I was free!

There was little hope of getting out of prison soon, but that was my obsession. There were many times that I considered the possibility of escape and even conspired with others and made plans. All of which had little chance of succeeding and were always rejected because I didn't know what I would do if it were successful. The thought of running for the rest of my life had absolutely no appeal. Besides, where could I run or hide? The reason I wanted out of jail was to be with my family, and I damn sure couldn't go home if I escaped.

The hopelessness of my situation generated a very strong desire in me to prevent it from ever happening to anyone else. I ached every day and felt the frustration of not knowing if the pain would ever cease. I was alive, bursting with energy, a newly acquired sense of freedom, and a desire to do something besides sit in a jail wasting away.

It's not hard to find someone who needs a shoulder to cry on in jail and oddly enough they aren't all inmates. I had made friends with some of the guards and spent a lot of time talking with them. Most prison guards like to think that they are "all right" with the inmates and will do just about anything to maintain the impression.

There are some officers who relate to the inmate population because they can't get along with fellow officers. These are the ones who never last very long. There is a "guards" mentality that's very hard for anyone other than a fellow idiot to relate to. I spent a lot of time talking to people and just as much time listening.

There was a riot at the Youth Center in Lorton, Virginia, and about sixty young kids from there were transferred to the jail. A special tier on the first floor was cleared out and used as maximum security to house them. These boys caused a lot of problems for the jail because they had to be kept separated from the rest of the inmates.

I had been working as the cell block clerk and had complete freedom to move about the block. The officer in charge was perfectly willing to let me take over all the clerical work. In exchange I was permitted certain privileges, like staying out of my cell, having my clothes pressed, showering whenever I pleased, having longer visits. My animosity toward the guards had almost completely gone and what little I had left was under control.

I spent a lot of time talking to the guys who were up from the Youth Center. I knew what it was like to be on lock-up. I was only twenty-one years old myself, but the past three years in jail had aged me far beyond my years. I had problems trying to figure out exactly what my role was at the jail. I was serving a life sentence but I didn't feel like an inmate. I didn't belong there, but I made no false pretenses about the fact that I was very much in jail. My feelings were very mixed. I couldn't identify with the inmate population; I wasn't trying to "figure out the next job," or impress

anyone about how successful I was on the streets, or talk
about all the whores I had working for me or how much
money I had made selling dope. At the same time, I
couldn't identify with the guards at all. One of the most
significant changes in my own attitude was probably my
realization that I had to relate to people on a human level
and not through any other means. Using this principle
solved a lot of problems for me and really gave me a solid
basis for judging people.

You'll find that people who are not decent human beings
to begin with make lousy everythings! It's a standing rule!

George Thomas had filed a notice of appeal and we were
again on the legal road.

We had become great friends by the time the second trial
ended. George had done everything he could to win the
case, but it was just too much to ask. We were certain to
have the case reversed on appeal. The trial judge had not
only refused to rule on certain issues, but when he did make
a ruling, there was no justification for his decisions—especially on the inadmissibility of the statements.

Like all institutions, the D.C. Jail had every ingredient
to make inmates antisocial. The frustration of confinement
brings out the animalistic instinct in man—makes him
harsh, cruel, brutal. It's tough not to be affected by it, but
it's possible. I had my taste of it and decided that I didn't
like the person it was making of me. I was already up to
my ass in trouble and I damn sure wasn't going to make
it tougher on myself. The only way to maintain some sem-
blance of sanity was to stay in touch with reality.

My outrage at what this society had done to me up to this
point as a black person was enough to refuse any further
indignities.

I had been labeled a murderer, which wasn't nearly as
offensive to me as being called a nigger! The Black Muslims
had given me a heavy dose of Blackness and I liked it. They

had also helped me to better understand my resentment for white people—which wasn't a resentment for white *people* at all, but more of a resentment and rejection of a white-oriented society which branded everything nonwhite as being nonworthy.

It was largely a matter of pride and anger that kept me from becoming a lost soul. Also there was my friendship with George. I liked him—trusted and respected him because he was just a damn good human being to begin with!

My mother had taken ill and was admitted to the D.C. General Hospital. I was considered a model prisoner by that time and was permitted to visit her on several occasions. It makes all the difference in the world to have someone depend on you. The jail couldn't take that away. My mother needed me and I would never let her down. We talked for hours about people and their relationships with each other. She was a born psychologist and understood human behavior much more than I realized.

From our talks, she was also getting to be quite a lawyer. She constantly encouraged me to take advantage of all the educational programs I could and to read everything printed. "You'd be surprised where you find knowledge," she kept saying. That was true, but I don't think she ever realized how much I had gotten from her.

I received a letter from the Clerk of the Court of Appeals informing me that Mr. Alfred V. J. Prather had been appointed to represent me on appeal. The letter also had his address and the firm he was with. Covington and Burling was undoubtedly one of the biggest and best law firms on the East Coast. They weren't into criminal law at all, but I figured you're better off with a large firm and their resources than with a topnotch criminal lawyer who does his own leg work.

George was going to remain on the case and help with the appeal, so it really didn't matter that Covington and

Burling wasn't widely reputed for its work in criminal matters.

I immediately wrote a letter to Mr. Prather giving him some information about the case and some of my ideas about how I thought we should proceed.

The first of many meetings with him was very encouraging. He was a loving, giving, compassionate man—qualities that are often all but nonexistent in lawyers.

Al Prather was also very frank. He had only been involved in one or two criminal cases before; his clients were serving time in Lorton, Virginia. How could any fighting man give up with two strikes against him. Al Prather had sporting blood. Before this case was over, he'd need every drop of it.

During the months of preparation for the appeal, Al and I didn't always talk about the case. We soon became friends and grew very close to each other. We'd talk about the jail, and he would always impress upon me the importance of trying to stay out of trouble. Al satisfied a lot of my emotional and intellectual needs and would visit me simply because I was concerned about something and needed someone to talk to. I received a great deal of moral support from Al Prather.

He believed that I was worth something and he would do everything he could to help me.

X

Enter Al

(Al)

The first I heard of Eddie Harrison and his troubles was on July 26, 1963. In my mail that morning was a letter from the Clerk of the United States Court of Appeals for the District of Columbia Circuit, enclosing an order appointing me to represent the appellant in Criminal Case No. 17991, *Eddie M. Harrison* vs. *United States.* Also enclosed were papers telling me how to proceed with a criminal case on appeal. The instructions were needed—I was a lawyer for corporations, partner in a large law firm, with limited knowledge of criminal law. In law school I had received the usual second-year course in criminal law twelve years earlier and had handled one previous criminal case by appointment of this same court. That was the sum total of my training and experience in criminal law. I was about to get more. A lot more.

If Eddie Harrison had walked into my office that morning and offered me a big fee to represent him, I would have refused. Our office did not take criminal cases. Our clients were mostly corporate giants; our work generally involved their problems with the federal government—an antitrust charge; a tax question; the regulatory proceedings of transport companies, radio and television broadcasters, and other industries. Of course Eddie would never have come to such a firm seeking counsel, and he would never have made it past the reception desk if he had tried. Nevertheless, the firm had a thriving criminal law practice, all of it nonpaying, all by appointment of the various courts. My appointment to represent Eddie was only one of many throughout an office numbering more than a hundred lawyers.

These appointments are made by the courts because the law says that a person accused of a criminal offense is entitled to the assistance of counsel at every step of the proceedings against him, and most people accused of crimes can't afford to hire a lawyer. The government provides lawyers to prosecute criminals but not, generally, to defend them, though some states have public defender systems under which the accused is given counsel if he cannot afford one of his own choosing. In the nation's capital, however, the courts supply counsel for indigent defendants by appointing private lawyers to represent them. Until recently, such appointed counsel served without compensation. Now they receive fees from the government, but the amounts are nominal, with a top limit of $500 even if the case takes thousands of dollars worth of the lawyer's time. In a small firm, or for a lawyer completely on his own, such an appointment can be disastrous financially if the lawyer really does a thorough job for the appointed client. Needless to say, some do not, and some find ways to get excused from the appointment. But many lawyers consider such appointments a professional responsibility and a trust, and stories of dedicated service by court-appointed counsel are legion.

Our firm prided itself on its record of service in appointed cases, many of which had become landmarks in the law. The younger lawyers, especially, considered a criminal appointment a challenge, and a stimulating change from normal practice. At least I did, and I know there were many others in the firm who felt the same way. So I was not dismayed at the appointment—I only hoped that it would be an interesting and worthwhile case. And I looked forward to seeing who this Eddie Harrison was and what he was like and what his case was all about.

It didn't take long to find out. The court had sent Eddie a letter informing him that I had been appointed to represent him, and he put me to work right away. On the same day I received the appointment, Eddie penned the first of many letters he was to send me in the next five years. He listed several steps that he thought should be taken in prosecuting his appeal and wanted me to come see him at my "earliest opportunity." He signed it with "advance thanks for your speedy reply." Eddie didn't know I was just clearing up my desk to go to the beach with my family for a badly needed vacation. And I didn't know that the vacation was to be greatly abbreviated. I went to see him.

It was my first visit to the D.C. Jail. I didn't even know where it was. The cab headed away from Washington's "little Wall Street" and turned down Constitution Avenue toward Capitol Hill. We sped past the Capitol Building and into the area beyond on the one route through the ghetto known to all suburban Washingtonians—the route to D.C. Stadium (now RFK Stadium), and the neighboring National Guard Armory, site of the International Horse Show, National Capital Flower Show, auto shows, and other such events. A predominately white area twenty years earlier when I was a high school student, it saw whites in number now only as they whisked through the sometimes narrow streets on their way to and from the stadium and the armory, wondering how anybody could have been stupid enough to build these places so far from the people who used them. It was a neighborhood many feared even to drive through, at least after dark.

As the cab threaded its way almost to the stadium, the driver asked which entrance to the jail I wanted. I didn't know. With a shrug he guessed that the visitors' entrance at 200 Nineteenth Street SE was my best bet.

The cab pulled to the curb in front of a large, red brick building, set back a few yards from the street and surrounded by high chain link fences topped with barbed wire. Looking at the building I was reminded of a humorous welcome to a large Midwestern university campus years earlier during a debating tournament, when the architecture of the older parts of the campus had been described as "early nineteenth-century American penitentiary." The description fit.

I stepped from the cab and looked around. Soaring in the background were the graceful white curves of the roof that covers the upper sections of the stands in D.C. Stadium. A little way up the one-way street, well-dressed Negro women stood waiting at a bus stop, their bright-eyed, smiling children frisking around them. Across the street were the tan brick row houses so familiar to Washington, with their white-pillared front porches commanding a view of the jail across the otherwise pleasant tree-lined street.

I turned toward the gate in the high fence. Between the street and the gate was a round brick tower, two stories tall, without windows except at the top. There a policeman in shirt sleeves sat perched in obvious discomfort in the muggy Washington heat. I walked over to the gate, which had no handles, and was confronted by what looked like a small, outdoor-type loudspeaker. A sign next to it read "State your business." Feeling slightly ridiculous to be talking to an anchor fence, I said that I was an attorney who had been appointed to represent one Eddie Harrison and that I wished to see him. The gate slid open and, as I stepped into the yard, slid shut promptly behind me.

Ahead of me a few yards were steps leading to a heavy, barred, metal door. Mounting them, I stood looking through thick glass at the top of the door into a room divided by a wooden divider similar to the tellers' stalls in a bank, topped by a heavy metal screen that went all the way to the ceiling. To the left, behind the screen, were desks and filing cabinets and two or three officers working —one sorting mail, another talking on the phone. Office routine is the same everywhere.

An officer touched a button and the electrically operated door opened with a loud buzzing signal. I entered and stated my business. The officer turned to a locator file and quickly found Harrison's card. Picking up the phone he called the cell block, ordered Eddie Harrison to be brought to the "rotunda," and said that I could go on in.

I turned to another heavy metal door with a thick glass window at the top. It had no knobs, and a sign on it cautioned me to be careful of my hands and feet because it was electrically operated. Again there was the buzzing signal and I stepped into a narrow, windowless, high-ceilinged corridor with a door at the opposite end, a few steps away, similar to the one I had just come through. The door closed behind me and I walked to the second door. There was a push button next to it, but a sign reserved it for official use only. I peered through the window into what was obviously the rotunda.

It was a huge enclosure—ballroom size—with a ceiling some four or five stories high. To the left was an office with a half dozen or so desks, sealed off from the rest of the room by a one-story ceiling and heavy walls, glass from the waist up. Around the walls of most of the rest of the room visible through the door were gray, solid metal cubicles not unlike rows of solid, doorless telephone booths. Each had a small, thick glass window, facing outward at eye level for someone sitting down. Next to each window was what looked like a wall phone without the dial, and facing each window was a shiny metal chair. Visiting booths.

The center of the room was filled with two long parallel rows of oblong, shiny-metal tables, placed end to end, with chairs on opposite sides, like a dining hall of some sort. To the right facing out on these rows of tables was a desk at which an officer sat shuffling papers, his broad unmoving back toward the door at which I stood. To his right were benches where a few blue-denimed prisoners sprawled, completely relaxed. High on the solid brick walls the gray monotony was broken by huge colorful murals with industrial themes, undoubtedly the work of a prisoner.

No one seemed to be aware of my presence, but eventually an officer with a bunch of keys on a chain at his waist strolled over and unlocked the door. I was waved to a seat at one of the long, shiny tables.

I noticed that a few other lawyers were spotted along these tables, talking with prisoners seated opposite them. A prison official sat at the head of the row of tables, interviewing a prisoner and noting answers on a long form. I looked over at the benches at the prisoners who were waiting to be interviewed, wondering whether one might be my new client. They were an unlikely looking lot, all seemingly unconcerned with where they were and disinterested in what was going on. Apparently none of them was Eddie Harrison, because my coming seemed to make no difference to them or to the officers strolling about or the people working in the cagelike office in the corner.

After a few minutes' wait, the officer with the keys went over to a door on the side of the room adjoining the visiting booths and opened it for a face peering out from the small window. A tall, slender, Negro youth stepped out and walked with the graceful step of a natural athlete toward the officer's desk. He bent over the desk to sign the form and, turning, followed the officer's pointing arm toward me at the table. Even as he walked, his dark eyes seemed to be sizing me up. His face—handsome, light-skinned, intelligent-looking—was immobile, seemingly emotionless. Even at first glance it was obvious that my new client was no ordinary jailbird.

Our conversation lasted for an hour or two, maybe more. Eddie sketched in for me the story of his case, speaking easily and well. He told me of the accidental killing, the false confessions and, surprisingly to me, the legal theories he thought applicable to his appeal. He spoke knowledgeably of recent decisions of the courts that he thought would be helpful to his case. He was especially interested in the Harling case, in which the Court of Appeals had recently held that a confession obtained from a juvenile could not be used against him if his case was transferred from the special juvenile court to the regular district court for trial as an adult, as Eddie's had been. He also felt sure he had good appeal arguments on grounds of double jeopardy and failure of speedy trial—two constitutional issues that he understood much better than I had when I entered law school. He had suggestions on tactics as well, wanting me to seek to have his appeal separated from those of Orson White and Joseph Sampson, his two co-defendants at the recently completed trial. He had a seemingly endless flow of ideas about how I should proceed, and I couldn't even hold up my end of the conversation. I could hardly tell him when or why he was right or wrong on most of them—he was much better versed on the subject than I was.

One thing I did know, and it disturbed me deeply. Eddie Harrison was flirting with death. He had been convicted of first-degree murder. For that he could have been sentenced to death. However, the jury had recommended a life sentence instead. What would be the effect of a successful appeal? I didn't know and there was no way to know. There were several possibilities:

Take first the double jeopardy point Eddie was urging on me. His argument was that his second trial never should have been held—that the Court of Appeals did not have the power to reverse his original conviction and send his case back for a second trial over his objection. The Constitution says that a man cannot be tried twice for the same offense. In the ordinary case the defendant waives that right when he takes an appeal. That is, by taking an appeal the defendant is asking the higher court to give him a second trial because of errors committed in his first. He doesn't receive the constitutional protection under the double jeopardy provision, only because he does not want it.

But Eddie had not asked for a second trial. The Court of Appeals had given him a chance to ask for one when it had discovered that his first trial was unfair, but he had refused. The court had appointed counsel to ask for a new trial for him and when the request came before Judge Matthews, Eddie renounced the request and objected to a new trial. He certainly had not waived his constitutional right to be tried but once, and the position of the government, expressed in a pleading filed at that time by the U.S. Attorney, was that a second trial should not be granted without such a waiver because Harrison would have a double jeopardy claim. Eddie Harrison's first conviction, they said, should not be reversed.

So there was considerable merit in Eddie's double jeopardy argument, but it carried one great problem. If the Court of Appeals lacked power to reverse his first conviction and order a second trial, his first conviction was still valid *and carried with it a sentence of death.* The argument boiled down to one that Eddie had a constitutional right to be executed rather than be tried twice. Some argument!

At the moment, sitting in the rotunda, I couldn't find a way around that problem. But Eddie was so dedicated to the point that I promised to explore it, and to argue it if at all possible. I could tell him what was wrong with the argument and of my fears concerning it, but I could not bring myself flatly to dismiss the point when he had paid so high a price to preserve it. He had spent eighteen months on Death Row refusing to ask for a new trial in what looked to me like a battle of wills with the government, while the Court of Appeals pondered what to do with so novel a question. The least I could do was give the argument a run for the money, even if it looked hopeless to me. Unless, of course, I couldn't find a way around the problem that winning the argument meant the electric chair for my client.

Eddie had an answer to that. He said he would rather take a chance of being put to death than give up a chance for freedom. He would rather be dead than without hope. He said that under a life sentence he could be eligible for parole in twenty years, but by then he would have lost the best years of his life and be an old man. His answer was understandable, coming from a twenty-one-year-old who had been imprisoned for three years.

Even without the double jeopardy argument, if I were to decide that it could not be made safely, Eddie was running the risk of another death sentence by taking an appeal. If the Court of Appeals were to upset the present conviction—which carried a life sentence recommended by the jury—and order a new trial, another jury might convict Eddie again and recommend the death penalty. Or, if the jury made no recommendations as to punishment, the judge might impose a death sentence.

Eddie understood that, but it didn't seem to bother him as it did me. He had an abiding faith in his case that would brook neither fear nor doubt. He definitely wanted to appeal, whether I thought he was risking death or not. It was, after all, his life. I couldn't argue with that.

Throughout the conversation, Eddie made frequent reference to the lawyer who had represented him at the second trial, George Thomas. He wanted me to talk to Mr. Thomas about the case because Mr. Thomas was an experienced criminal lawyer for whom Eddie had a great deal of respect. It became increasingly clear, as my own inexpertness unfolded, that Eddie would feel a lot better about things if Mr. Thomas could be brought into the case on appeal. Mr. Thomas was a fighting lawyer and a real man, who knew all the ins and outs of the criminal law and of this complicated case. Eddie believed he would be very helpful.

I had never met George Thomas or heard of him, though I later found out that he was a well-known defense counsel in criminal cases here in the District. But I was encouraged to learn that Eddie had been represented by someone he liked, trusted, and did not blame for his conviction. Many prisoners who have been represented by court-appointed lawyers are quick to turn on them after conviction, and not a few appeals have been based on a claim that the prisoner's court-appointed counsel was incompetent or not diligent in his defense. It was good to know that Eddie believed in his trial counsel and thought Mr. Thomas would be willing to help on the appeal. I promised to see him right away.

Our conversation finished, Eddie went back to his cell and I went out through the same labyrinth of doors through which I had entered. Outside the sun was shining brightly, and it suddenly struck me that I could remember no windows in the high-ceilinged rotunda. Actually there were a few—way up high—but on that first visit they had gone unnoticed. As the door to the jail buzzed shut behind me, I felt a surprisingly urgent need to be beyond the gate ahead of me. The guard in the tower saw me coming and the gate slid open as I approached it. I smiled and waved to him. It felt good to be outside again.

Hailing a cab, I went to see George Thomas. He was a "Fifth Street" lawyer with an office in the Century Building—a very different breed of cat from the "uptown" lawyer from Fifteenth Street. Separated by only ten blocks, the working worlds of the two groups were as far apart as different planets. Fifth Street borders the several-block string of buildings that house the various Washington courts, beginning with the Juvenile Court and the Municipal Court and pyramiding through various branches and levels to their apex, the United States Court of Appeals for the District of Columbia Circuit. At that time the latter was the ultimate court of appeal—short of the Supreme Court of the United States—for all of these courts as well as for most decisions of federal agencies such as the Civil Aeronautics Board, the Atomic Energy Commission, the Federal Communications Commission. The Court of Appeals—and the annual banquet of the Bar Association of the District of Columbia—were about the only common meeting grounds of most "Fifth Street" and "uptown" lawyers, and even here they found little in common. I remember one of the Bar Association banquets I attended where the entertainment included a series of skits lampooning various aspects of practice in the local courts. It was hilarious to the Fifth Street crowd, but the uptown crowd rarely knew what was going on.

I felt that way now as I walked into the Century Building. An oldish office building, small and bedraggled, it was one of the two best on Fifth Street, which otherwise consisted mostly of houses converted into offices, store-front restaurants, and bail bondsmen's shops. No corporate vice-presidents frequented these halls, and pretentious quarters would have been out of place. For here, close to the courtrooms to which they scurried on hectic, unmanageable schedules, were the men who knew all that I did not. Here came those accused of crime or, more often, their families, when a criminal lawyer was needed. Not all who practiced in the criminal courts were here, of course. There was, I knew, a heavy concentration of Negro lawyers farther up on Sixth and Seventh Streets, who were regulars in the criminal courts, and there were others scattered at various points in the city, including uptown. But here was the

stronghold of the backbone troops in the classic courtroom
battles for the rights of the accused. These were the men
who knew how to "shop" to get their man before a lenient
judge, when to dicker with the government to get accept-
ance of a plea to a lesser offense, which jurors to challenge
out of the jury box and which ones to keep. If they were
not all Perry Masons, many of them were his betters because they frequently were successful, partially or completely, in defending someone who seemed to be guilty
beyond doubt, while Mason had to go to prodigious
lengths to defend clients who always turned out to be quite
innocent.

As a group they were aging, for many had fallen from
their ranks in recent years and few young lawyers these
days wanted to fill their places. Theirs was a demanding
practice that rarely produced a decent fee and frequently
produced none. It was no place for a man to get rich, and
who didn't want to get rich?

George Thomas, that's who. He was younger than most
of the others—perhaps any other—in the Fifth Street conclave. I liked him as soon as I saw him, and I suppose most
everyone did. Short, but with a solid breadth that made him
seem a larger man than he really was, George wore the
rugged map of Greece on his face. A ready smile and wrin-
kles all headed in the right direction bespoke a kindliness
I later often saw demonstrated. He had—and has—a natural, old-country courtesy surpassing that of anyone I have
ever known. Small wonder Eddie Harrison trusted and respected this man. I did, too, at once, instinctively. He was
a man to reckon with, I was to learn. He dearly loved courtroom battle, genuinely respected friend and foe there alike
unless and until they proved themselves unworthy, and was
totally without illusions, without being in the least cynical.

When he learned that I was Eddie's lawyer for the appeal,
he welcomed me to a corner of his desk and was soon
telling me all about Eddie, the trial, the points he thought

could be appealed. It had been a rousing trial from beginning to end. He had known almost from its outset that Eddie had no chance of acquittal and acccordingly had bent his efforts toward appeal, objecting to everything possible. There had been much to object to. The judge who had presided over Eddie's trial was famous throughout the land as a legal scholar with strong opinions. These were affected not at all by the views of the Court of Appeals or the Supreme Court, though he was bound to follow their decisions and, where there was no other way out, did so in spite of contrary convictions, but with obvious and vocal distaste. He was notoriously tough on defendants he believed guilty but could be equally tough on prosecutors when he thought the occasion called for it or he believed the defendant innocent. His judicial attitude was reflected at many points in the Harrison trial, but nowhere more clearly than in his ruling admitting the crucial confession that was to lead to Eddie's conviction.

The transcript follows:

> The Court: Now, I want to say to you gentlemen that it had been my view that the Mallory case does not apply to juveniles. . . .
>
> However, strangely enough—it seems strange to me—the Court of Appeals in the Harling case held that the Mallory case does apply to a juvenile. . . .
>
> I think this is a very close case. The Mallory case, anyway, is an artificial rule; it does not relate to constitutional rights at all; it only attaches a consequence, an adverse consequence as a result of a violation of a rule of procedure.
>
> You know, in trying a criminal case a trial judge has to be cognizant of the fact that the government has no appeal. If I exlude [sic] this and if I hold that the Harling case applies, the government has no way of securing a review of my ruling, and there may be a miscarriage of justice.

On the other hand, if I admit this and the Court of Appeals disagrees with me—I do not say, if I am wrong; I think I will be right in admitting it, but the Court of Appeals has a right to disagree with me, and they have the last say.

It is just like a baseball umpire, if he calls a strike a ball it counts as a ball even though it is a strike.

If the Court of Appeals then disagrees with me there will be an appellate review.

Mr. Smithson: That is correct, sir.

The Court: Whereas, if I decided against the government there is no opportunity for an appellate review.

Now, I myself feel, and my own opinion is, that the Harling case should be confined to its strict facts, because of the rather unusual situation.

I think the interests of logic and justice would require the admission of this statement, and while I appreciate that the objection is not a frivolous one, one that is worthy of consideration, I am going to overrule it.

George thought this ruling was erroneous and that Eddie's appeal would be successful. He thought little of Eddie's double jeopardy and speedy trial arguments, but agreed that they should be included in the appeal because they had at least a faint chance for success and one should never presume to prejudge the Court of Appeals. He readily volunteered to assist me in any way he could, and was sure Eddie's conviction would be reversed because he was convinced the trial had been unfair. Like Eddie, he was unafraid of possible imposition of the death penalty if Eddie had to go to trial a third time. He said that no jury on earth could sit through a trial looking at a handsome young fellow like Eddie and send him to his death for a killing that even a tough prosecutor had said was accidental. "Believe me," he said, and I did. But I was never to lose the faint fear that haunted me from time to time throughout the case. What if we were wrong?

Leaving my new ally, I returned to the office, grabbing a sandwich on the way. The day was little more than half gone, but it seemed years since I had left my desk to go to the jail that morning. I felt distracted and unable to concentrate on the mail before me. The routine of my regular work, so vital just hours before, seemed dull, lifeless, and unimportant. I kept thinking of Eddie in jail and George down on Fifth Street and I felt out of it. I had glimpsed a world I knew nothing about, and my appetite for exploration and eventual conquest was whetted. I was hooked on this case and I knew it. Some cases are like that. Or some lawyers.

XI

Lewisburg

(*Eddie*)

After spending about four years in the D.C. Jail, and just before the second appeal was filed, I was informed that I was being transferred to the Federal Penitentiary at Lewisburg, Pennsylvania. The notice came as a shock to me. I had never considered being transferred to a penitentiary because I had never seriously considered serving the sentence. Somewhat panic-stricken, I called one of the jail captains to see what could be done to stop the order. It was not a good time for me to be going to Lewisburg. My mother was still seriously ill and needed me close to her. It would be too much for her if I were shipped off to some penitentiary. I knew all too well how difficult it was to get out of a federal prison once you are sent there. By far the most frightening part was to be moved out of the legal jurisdiction, to be away from the courts and not have constant knowledge of what's going on. There wasn't very much that I could do about it, though.

I did get a chance to talk to my mother and Al before

I left. They both felt it would be only for a short period; in no more than six months the case would be reversed and either dismissed or sent back to the District Court for retrial.

The six months I expected to be in Lewisburg slowly stretched into two and a half agony-filled years. It's very easy to lose yourself in the ever-moving stream of humanity. It seemed like the only purpose was to keep moving.

The sleeping and eating quarters were in the same building. A loudspeaker system shouted orders like a traffic cop at a busy intersection. Lewisburg had one black correctional officer on its staff—that was typical of the institutional philosophy. I was a loner and I felt like an intruder. Everyone had to work at Lewisburg and I was no exception. I thought I had myself pretty well together when I entered there, but I had to fight constantly to maintain my own feelings of self-worth and dignity.

I had three strikes against me when I entered Lewisburg. I was a convicted murderer serving a life sentence, a Washingtonian, and black. In all institutions, prisoners from the District of Columbia are considered troublemakers because they stick together. Most of the fights in Lewisburg involved the "D.C. boys." It was a standing rule among the inmates not to fuck around with the D.C. boys.

I was expected to maintain this pattern or be rejected by the group. I felt the group pressure on a number of occasions but somehow always managed gracefully to find a way out of it by hiding behind my sentence. In Lewisburg my individuality was systematically assaulted. I was willing to work, but they were not interested in what I *wanted* to do. To the prison assignment board I was just an answer to their manpower shortage. First in the laundry and then in the press department of the federal prison industries complex. I soon discovered that the only way to exist in prison was to live one day at a time and just try to survive. The prison library was my sanctuary. There wasn't any law material in the library and my personal law books had to be kept on "deposit" in the library. All of my legal papers had to be kept in the library, and I was only permitted to use them during library hours. Inmates were not permitted to share their law books and could be punished if caught doing so. Nor were inmates permitted to help each other file petitions or writs.

Racial disturbances were frequent in Lewisburg. Most of the guards were local townspeople who had little or no knowledge of how to deal with inmates, black or white. They were mostly farmers who were programmed to work in the prison for lack of any other available jobs in the rural Lewisburg area. Most of them were of the "turnkey" mentality, who saw their job mostly in terms of keeping the prisoners under lock and key and exercising total authority over their lives. The guards were the cause of most of the unrest in the institution and there was no escape from their constant harassment. It seemed like they were waiting for you at every turn.

The more pressure they put on me, the more I was determined to resist. I received constant assurances from Al that the court would reach its decision soon, and this gave me additional strength. I tried to develop a program that kept me from coming into contact with the guards as much as possible. I worked, studied, and took my frustrations out on the basketball court.

Archie lived on the same floor as I did, and we got to be pretty good buddies. He was one of the few friends I had while in Lewisburg. I had learned to play the guitar and Archie wanted me to teach him. It was a strange friendship at first. Archie was white and that indicated to the guards that he was a homosexual. Most of the black/white relationships were homosexual, and for that reason few blacks and whites got to be friends.

The sexual issue has become the basis for racism in the country as a whole, and it was that way in the institutions.

Most racist whites cringe at the thought of some black man fucking a white woman, and in prison it boils the guts of the guards to know that blacks are also fucking white men!

Archie was called to the captain's office and told to "stay away from that nigger if you know what's good for you." Archie was far from being a homosexual and resented being called into the captain's office. He even got away with calling the captain a "red-neck motherfucker" while leaving his office.

I wrote letters to the director of the Federal Bureau of Prisons requesting a transfer back to Washington, but never received an answer. My trust in Al Prather and George Thomas was the only thing that kept me from being completely demoralized. If it were not for the security of knowing that somewhere in D.C. there was a man pushing my appeal through the legal machinery, I would have been like the other lifers in Lewisburg—without hope, without any conception of freedom, decency, or self-respect.

My mother had become critically ill and I was powerless to do anything about it. I noticed how consistently weak and scratchy her handwriting was getting. I tried to arrange a visit to the hospital, but such procedures were all but nonexistent. She was dying; still I was her main concern. I assured her that I was all right and would be home soon. My words had more meaning to her than they did to me. I wasn't sure when I would leave this place; I only knew that I was going to.

It wasn't in time to be of any relief to my mother. She died before I had a chance to make amends for all the pain I had caused her.

The institution chaplain called me to his office and broke the news. My stepfather had called the institution but they would not permit him to talk to me.

I was completely heartbroken and it was one of the few times that I lost control of myself. My caseworker told me that I was not going to be permitted to attend my mother's funeral. Without thinking about what I was saying, I told him that he was either going to let me go or I was going to find a way to get there on my own. He told me to go back to work and I told him to go to hell and left his office.

Shortly after our conversation, I was called back into his office and told that I would be permitted to return to Washington for the funeral.

While in Washington I also had a chance to talk to Al. There was absolutely nothing that could be done to speed up the Court of Appeals. The only thing to do was wait until they made up their minds. It was good to see Al—no, I hadn't lost any hope. We were surely going to win this case and I could hold out, if the court didn't dismiss the indictment outright. Surely they would rule the "confessions" out and there would be no case anyway, so we'd be in good shape no matter what happened!

Maxine and I had lost touch during the last year or so. It was close to four years now since I had been arrested. She was having a lot of problems that I just couldn't help her with. Two children to care for alone is quite a responsibility—she had physical and emotional needs that I obviously couldn't respond to. I was permitted to see her at the jail before being transferred back to Lewisburg. She hadn't changed much at all. Still the same devoted, trusting, ever-loving girl I had left four years earlier. Shockingly similar to the way I left her four years earlier, even down to her pregnancy! No wonder she hadn't bothered to visit me at Lewisburg after being put on my visiting list!

I felt some bitterness toward her and refused to see her anymore. I could rationalize and understand how she might have made the mistake of getting pregnant, but I couldn't dismiss the intense feeling of being betrayed. Nor did I feel I could trust her again. Both these feelings would pass in time.

It was a long quiet ride back to Lewisburg. I enjoyed the quietness; it gave me an opportunity to try and decide what to replace the empty pieces of me with.

XII

Six to Four

(AI)

The first step in preparing an appeal—especially in a case where someone else handled the actual trial—is to read the court reporter's transcript of the trial, which is a verbatim record of everything that was said there. That's where the facts are buried and where the errors must be found. There's a volume of transcript for every day of the trial, and in Eddie's case there were many volumes. I started reading.

Eddie's side of the story was all there, substantially as he had told it to me at the jail. But so was the government's side of the case, and it was highly convincing. There were signed confessions by all three defendants, admitting that they had gone to Brown's house to rob him. Eddie's confession admitted the actual killing. Though the killing was accidental—and the government did not contend otherwise—it was first-degree murder because of the so-called "felony murder" rule. Under that rule any killing which occurs during a robbery or attempted robbery (or certain other crimes), whether accidental or intentional, is first-degree murder; otherwise an accidental killing is a lesser crime, or not a crime at all, depending on the circumstances. If Eddie's story that he went to Brown's house to pawn his shotgun was true, he was not guilty of first-degree murder. If on the other hand, the confession that he went to Brown's house to rob him was true, he had been rightly convicted of first-degree murder under the felony murder rule.

Which version of the facts was true made no difference to me. Whether guilty or innocent, Eddie was my client by appointment of the court, and it was my job to fight for him. It was the business of the courts and the U.S. Attorney's office to see that justice was done. It was my business to get Eddie out of jail, if that was legally possible.

I was not overly impressed by the fact that the police had obtained a confession. In the only other criminal case I had handled, the police had confessions from six teenage Negro boys that they had raped a white woman, though one of the six had in fact not even been within miles of the scene. Think of that! They could have convicted that boy of a capital offense he had nothing to do with, and they might have, if the truth hadn't been discovered. How could a thing like that happen? It probably couldn't any more, but that was before the Miranda case, when the police were able to question suspects in a back upstairs room at the precinct station in the wee hours of the morning, far away from lawyers and magistrates. In that case, as here, the defendants claimed they had signed confessions because they were being beaten. The NAACP had started an investigation of the charge but dropped the whole business when they found out that the officer accused of beating the boys was also Negro. But that's another story.

In any event, the mere existence of Eddie's confession didn't prove to me that he was guilty, particularly when the transcript showed that Eddie had told the truth about a key circumstance of the confession and the policeman who had obtained the confession had not.

Eddie said that he had signed the typewritten confession admitting attempted robbery because he was threatened. He said there were two policemen with him, one typing and the other questioning him, that the one typing got up and walked away for a few minutes, leaving Eddie alone with the officer who told him he would take him to the "hole" and "beat his ass" if he didn't sign. The officer Eddie accused testified that no such thing ever happened and that he had never been alone with Eddie. The officer at the typewriter backed up Eddie's story: he testified that he had in fact walked away and left Eddie and the questioning officer alone for a few minutes. That didn't prove that Eddie was threatened as he said, but it made me wonder. Why had the officer lied?

For purposes of the appeal, though, it didn't matter whether the confession was true, or whether it had been obtained by threats. These were questions of fact, and questions of fact are for the jury to decide, not the Court of Appeals. When the jury found Eddie guilty, that was that so far as the facts were concerned, and what I had to do was find some legal error—some reason why that confession should not have been admitted into evidence and gone to the jury. Of course *any* serious error I could find would get Eddie a new trial, but that wouldn't mean a thing if I couldn't get rid of the confession. Juries in the District almost always convict in any event, but there's no doubt they'll convict if there's a confession in evidence. So the question was, how could I get Eddie's conviction reversed and the confession declared unusable?

Eddie had given me the answer during that first interview at the D.C. Jail. The Harling case. George Thomas had contended at Eddie's trial that this case precluded use of Eddie's confession. George was sure the Court of Appeals would uphold his contention, but I was dubious.

149

The argument was this. At the time of the killing, Eddie was seventeen years old. Accordingly, he was at that time subject to the jurisdiction of the Juvenile Court, which has the exclusive right to handle all charges against anyone under the age of eighteen at the time of the offense. The Juvenile Court can waive its jurisdiction in certain cases, sending the defendant on to be tried in regular District Court as an adult would be, and that course was eventually taken in Eddie's case. That's the usual course in murder cases or other very weighty charges, because the Juvenile Court can't keep its defendants in prison beyond age twenty-one, when they cease to be juveniles. The lesson of the Harling case in such a situation was this: statements obtained from a juvenile while he was in the custody of officials who handle juvenile cases could not be used against him if the Juvenile Court waived jurisdiction over him and sent him on to be tried as an adult in the District Court. Once the case was sent to the regular District Court, it was a new ball game.

The reason for this rule was simple, and it is fair enough. The law provides strict procedural safeguards for adults accused of crime. They must be taken before a judicial official promptly after arrest, advised of the nature of the charge against them and of their right not to answer questions, warned that any answers they give can be used against them at their trial, and provided a lawyer if they do not have one. At the time of the Harling decision these protections were not afforded to juveniles, though they are today, more or less. At that time a juvenile had *no* right really, because he was not technically involved in a criminal case at all unless and until the Juvenile Court sent him on to trial in the District Court. So long as the Juvenile Court retained jurisdiction, the juvenile was sent to the Receiving Home for Children, not the D.C. Jail, and the effort was to reform him, not to punish him for a crime. The Juvenile Court was his friend, trying to help him, a sort of governmental "parent" that was really on his side and not neutral as an adult court is. Everything was very informal in dealing with juveniles, and they were encouraged to tell their side of the story, not warned as adults are that they are entitled to remain silent and that their failure to do so might produce damaging evidence for use against them at a trial. In these circumstances, the court had reasoned in the Harling case, it was unfair and a breach of trust to let statements obtained from a juvenile be used against him later if the Juvenile Court waived jurisdiction and sent him on to trial as an adult.

The trouble with trying to apply the Harling case rule to Eddie's case was that he wasn't in the hands of the juvenile authorities at the time he confessed, and he wasn't a juvenile. He was an adult and he was in the D.C. Jail, convicted of driving a speeding car without a license on his eighteenth birthday, just ten days after the Cider Brown killing. How could I hope to get the court to apply the rule of the Harling case to Eddie when the reasoning of the Harling case didn't apply to him? It didn't look like much of an argument to me. And since I didn't think there was a very good chance of winning his other two points—double jeopardy and speedy trial—I went over and over the trial transcript looking for other possible errors. I found only one more point worth arguing, and that point, even if successful, would merely lead to another trial at which the confession would be admissible and Eddie would presumably be convicted again. Eddie really had a lousy case. With little hope of doing Eddie much good, I turned to writing the brief to be submitted on his behalf to the Court of Appeals.

I was not alone in that effort. You never are if you're a partner in a big law firm—you always have help. Mine was extraordinarly good help because we never hired anyone who wasn't tops. My two helpers were Chuck Miller and Tom Donovan. The three of us represented what a small-town lawyer from the Midwest had once told me was the perfect law firm—a Protestant, a Jew, and an Irish Catholic. Tom was low man on the totem pole, being the newest associate in the firm, so he did all the dirty work—researching the obscure points of law, checking transcript and case citations, filling in references—all the things that a good lawyer wants done accurately and well but hates to do himself because they're a boring pain. Chuck was the "right hand" or "brains" of the operation. No partner in a first rate big law firm would even say "hello" to a client without a bright young man at his side to make sure he wasn't goofing the whole bit. Chuck was eminently qualified for that role. Suave and sophisticated almost to a fault, a former law clerk to a Supreme Court justice, familiar enough to tell me to go to hell at the drop of a hat if he thought I was wrong but wise enough to humor me along if that was called for, Chuck was a tower of strength.

Tom and Chuck did the basic legal research—mostly Tom, I suspect—digging through cases that might be helpful or harmful to our cause. I concentrated on the facts. My theory has always been that nothing else is terribly important in most law cases. If you can get the court to want to decide in your favor, they'll accept your legal reasoning easily enough, or even find legal reasons of their own to do it. But if they don't want to decide in your favor, they can be equally ingenious in finding legal reasons why your case is no good. The trick is to try to find some reason for them to want to decide in your favor, and the place to find that is in the facts of the case. The judges know the law, and most of them have pretty set ideas about it that lawyers arguing a cases before them aren't likely to change. What they don't know are the facts, and here the lawyer has his big opportunity and his principal function. He has to sell his case to the judges just as any salesman sells a product to a prospective buyer, and he has to do it with facts. As any salesman knows, the facts are what you make them, but only within limits. You can tell a man until you're blue in the face that a Volkswagen is beautiful, but he isn't going to be taken in if he has eyes. But you might be able to persuade him that looks aren't really the important thing, and that a Volks is just what he needs because of its economy. And it's the same problem in arguing a case. You can't change the facts in the printed transcript of the trial, but you should be able to persuade the Appellate Court that some facts are a lot more important than others. So that's what I set out to do: to find in that transcript some factual basis for persuading the court that justice had not been done. Because that's what the courts really care about—justice.

And that was the big problem with Eddie's case. It looked as if he'd gotten just what he had coming to him. He admitted he'd killed Brown, and there was a signed confession saying the killing had occurred during an attempted robbery. He claimed the confession was false, but the jury hadn't believed him and that settled the matter. There was the Harling case saying that confessions obtained from juveniles couldn't be used against them at an adult trial, but Eddie had been an adult, not a juvenile, when the police had obtained his confession. Where was any injustice? Where was the magic argument that would sell the court on the idea that it ought to reverse the conviction and exclude Eddie's confession from evidence?

Such arguments are usually made, not born. With me they're made of pacing the floor or staring out the window with unseeing eyes, or gazing at the ceiling with my feet on the desk, unconsciously lighting one cigarette after another while I try out one idea after another. I spend hours that way when the going is tough, and I'm impatient, irritable, and annoyed by interruptions. If you doubt it, ask anyone who's ever walked into my office when I'm in the midst of thinking through a case. It's hard on me and it's hard on everyone around me and I wish it weren't that way but it is. And the funny thing about it is that the idea that finally emerges is always so simple that any boob should have seen it right away without even thinking twice.

It was that way this time. Eddie had an argument that was almost irresistible. It was as obvious as the nose on your face, and it finally came to me. The whole argument was right there in the transcript at the point where the judge and the prosecutor were discussing whether Eddie's confession should be admitted, after George Thomas had objected on grounds that the Harling case barred its use. The prosecutor explained to the judge that at the time the confession had been obtained Eddie was an adult, having just turned eighteen, and so was not entitled to the protection afforded juveniles by the Harling case rule.

"Very well," said the judge in the transcript, "suppose he was entitled to be treated as an adult."

The prosecutor responded: "He wasn't as to the crime until Juvenile Court waived on him, Your Honor. They had to waive before we could have charged him."

The transcript continued:

> The Court: Of course hindsight is always better than foresight. It might have been better if they had waited until the waiver before they went down and talked to him at the jail.
>
> Mr. Smithson: Your Honor, I really can't say that, because they knew he was then an adult.
>
> The Court: He was what?
>
> Mr. Smithson: He was over the age of eighteen.
>
> The Court: Let us assume he was an adult. Then he should have been brought before a magistrate, should he not?
>
> Mr. Smithson: But not for a crime committed while he was a juvenile.

154

There it was in the transcript and I'd read it a dozen times and it bothered me right along, but I hadn't been able to quite put my finger on what was wrong before. At the time the confession was obtained, the government was saying, Harrison was at a most awkward age—too young to be given the protection afforded adults, too old to be given the protection afforded juveniles, and hence not entitled to protection at all. The Court of Appeals could never sit still for that. If Harrison was considered a juvenile, his confession was inadmissible under the Harling case. If he was considered an adult, his confession was inadmissible because he had not been taken before a magistrate and advised of the charge against him and his rights before the confession was obtained. He had to be considered one or the other and that's all there was to it. I just didn't see how he could lose. The confession was a dead letter in my mind from then on. I was sure I could get rid of it.

The other arguments still had to be worried out, especially the double jeopardy point. But Chuck Miller solved that one neatly enough. The record of the case in the office of the Clerk of the United States Court of Appeals showed that the impostor, "L. A. Harris," who represented Eddie at the end of the first trial, had filed a notice of appeal. That action gave the Court of Appeals jurisdiction to reverse the conviction, and its doing so had destroyed the death sentence that went with that conviction. But the filing of the notice of appeal could not serve as a waiver of Eddie's constitutional right not to be tried twice for the same crime, because an imposter who was not a lawyer could not waive his client's rights. So, we could go ahead and argue the double jeopardy point without seeming to be asking the court to send our client back to Death Row. It was no longer the risky argument it had seemed at first, but it still wasn't one calculated to appeal to the court. No judge was likely to turn a twice-convicted murderer loose because of error at his trial that could readily be corrected (and had been) by giving him a new trial. And if we were going to claim the benefit of the impostor's action in filing that notice of appeal, we were going to have a hard time persuading the court that we shouldn't take the detriment too, and have his action considered a request for a new trial by Eddie.

As it turned out, we had a hard time persuading the court of anything. We drew a tough bench. The United States Court of Appeals for the District of Columbia Circuit has nine judges. They sit on cases in panels of three, and it makes all the difference in the world which three judges you get to sit on your case. As on any court, the views of the judges varied widely. Some of them had very liberal views of criminal law. These judges, highly sensitive to the rights of those accused of crime, were receptive to arguments of procedural error. They did not hesitate to reverse convictions on the basis of "technicalities" of the law, because they believed that these procedural safeguards were vastly important to human liberty, the bulwark protecting the individual against the otherwise overwhelming power of the state. Other judges, more concerned with the victims of crime than with those accused of committing it, were determined not to let the guilty go free. The differing views of the judges produced a running debate from case to case, with different three-judge panels producing opposite decisions in seemingly very similar cases. And rare was the important criminal case that was not decided 2 to 1, with a sometimes stinging dissenting opinion.

There's no way to pick your judges, "shopping" for a bench that you think will be favorably inclined to your case. The panels are determined by lot; you get who you get and there's absolutely nothing you can do about it. In fact, you can't even find out in advance of the oral argument who your three judges are to be. On the morning of the argument the marshal raps his gavel, everyone in the courtroom stands up while he intones his "Oyez, oyez, oyez, the honorable the United States Court of Appeals for the District of Columbia Circuit is now in session," and out step three judges.

When our three entered and took their big black seats behind the long judicial bench, my heart sank. We had drawn two "conservatives" and one "liberal" by my assessment. I glanced at the U.S. Attorney seated at the next table. His confident smile confirmed my opinion that his opposition was in for rough going. The presiding judge called the case and and we were off.

In an oral argument in the Court of Appeals the appellant's lawyer speaks first. He is supposed to "state the case," telling the court briefly what the facts are before arguing the legal points. In the D.C. Circuit, however, the judges are familiar with the facts before the argument because they read the briefs submitted by the parties in advance, and it is their practice to advise counsel of that fact at the outset of an argument so he won't waste time telling them a lot of things they already know. There isn't much time, because the court normally allots only an hour to a case—half for the appellant and half for the government. The appellant is permitted to make a rebuttal after the government has argued, but he has to save the time for that rebuttal out of his original time allotment. So it's very helpful to have the court already familiar with the case, especially one with a long history like this one, where it would take most of the argument time just to state the facts.

I don't remember too much about the argument that morning—it's blurred in with too many others. But I remember one incident. At the outset I referred to Eddie as a lad. One of the judges interrupted, asking what it was this "lad" had done, whether he hadn't blown a man's head off with a shotgun. The tone of the question left no doubt of the conclusion to which the judge's study of the case had led him. Score one sure vote for the government. Not too

157

bothersome—I'd written him off as a possible vote for Eddie the minute he'd stepped into court anyway.

But even with a tough bench, there was going to be a reversal of some sort in the case. It wasn't just one case. Sampson and White had appealed too, and all three cases had been consolidated for argument and decision; this is the usual course followed where there are simultaneous appeals from convictions at trials involving more than one defendant. So there were three lawyers in court seeking to upset the case, one representing each man. The other two were also court-appointed uptown lawyers with little experience in criminal law—one was a labor lawyer, the other, a Federal Communications Commission expert. Their cases were, of course, quite similar to mine, with the critical exception that Sampson and White had not been juveniles at the time of the killing—and they had not held the gun. According to the government's argument, Sampson was the driver, down the street waiting in the get-away car, White was the look out man, staying out front to warn Eddie if anyone came along during the robbery. The argument was supported by signed confessions. When they signed those confessions, Sampson and White didn't know, I'm sure, that they were confessing to first-degree murder and sentencing themselves to death by electrocution. But they were, because under the felony murder rule it's not just the one who does the killing who's guilty of first-degree murder; it's everybody who participated in the attempted robbery; and the death sentence was mandatory in first-degree murder cases at that time.

However, it was clear that the Sampson and White confessions were going to be thrown out because they had been improperly obtained. Sampson and White had testified that the confessions had been beaten out of them by the police. The police testified that the claim was false and that their questioning of Sampson and White had been peaceable. The jury had convicted under instructions that they were to disregard the confessions if they found that they had been involuntary. Juries always seem to resolve such disputes in favor of the police; at least I never heard of a jury doing otherwise, and there were an awful lot of cases in which claims of police brutality were made in those days. I always figured such claims were frequently exaggerated or false; on the other hand I didn't doubt that sometimes the claims were true. If the police suspected me of murder, I am confident they'd be careful of my rights and there'd be no question of their mistreating me. But sassy teenage blacks from the wrong section of town with juvenile records—that's another thing, and I have no doubt that more than one of them has been slapped around—and worse—by tough cops. In fact I once heard a former prosecutor telling about the "good old days" when they used to sometimes "hang a smart-alecky nigger out the third floor window, head down. That loosened their tongues in a hurry!"

Maybe you don't think that matters—after all we live on the edge of a jungle full of preying beasts who would just as soon stick a knife in you as look at you, and if the cops don't treat the bad-actors with kid gloves, what the hell, would *you?*

The trouble is, how can you tell a "good nigger" from a bad one—and what makes you think a "bad nigger" doesn't have the same rights you do? "A man's a man for a' that," Bobbie Burns said, and you'd better believe it. If you don't, you're as guilty of the rioting and burning as the guys down there at Fourteenth and U with the torches, and you'd better wake up because that's what's happening, baby, and if you don't believe me ask your teenage kids because they know a lot more about it than you do and a lot of them care.

And so do the courts. That's why I knew we were going to win some kind of a reversal this morning in the Court of Appeals, even with a conservative bench. It was perfectly clear that the Sampson and White confessions had been illegally obtained even if the police never laid a finger on them. That was because of the famous—or infamous, depending on your point of view—Mallory case. There the Supreme Court had said that confessions obtained during an unnecessary delay between arrest and preliminary hearing could not be used in a criminal trial in federal courts. It wasn't a constitutional point, but was based on a statute. The congressionally prescribed criminal procedure at that time provided that when a man was arrested he was to be taken before a judicial official without "unnecessary delay." One of the objectives of that procedure was to advise a man of his constitutional right to remain silent and to have counsel. In the Mallory case the Supreme Court said that the police ought to obey that law exactly as it was written. They should take the prisoner to his preliminary hearing without "unnecessary delay," not take him to headquarters for questioning to try to get a confession and, having succeeded, then take him to court to be told that he didn't have to talk and get a lawyer who would surely warn him not to. If the police weren't going to obey the law, how could we expect that there would be any respect for law and order? The court couldn't run around policing the police, but they could make sure prosecutors and defense lawyers did.

The Mallory case had given rise to a lot of confusion because different judges had different ideas about what was an "unnecessary delay" and about the applicability of the Mallory doctrine to situations where the case wasn't squarely on point. For instance, what if a prisoner made a second, confirming confession *after* he had been given a preliminary hearing, but the confession obviously stemmed from the fact that he had let the cat out of the bag during an "unnecessary delay" before the preliminary hearing? There was room for honest disagreement on this and a host of other questions raised by the Mallory decision. Cases were going both ways all over the place, with some judges extending the doctrine of the case broadly to cover any situation they thought within its spirit and others applying the doctrine grudgingly and only where there was no room for doubt that they had to.

But in our case it was perfectly clear that some illegally obtained confessions had been used, and the government in its brief had "confessed error," admitting that Sampson was entitled to a new trial in their view because he had been interrogated too long before he was given a preliminary hearing. They defended the use of White's confession on grounds that it had not been occasioned by an unnecessary delay between arrest and preliminary hearing but "came immediately upon his being confronted with the accusatory story of a co-defendant," Sampson. And they saw no merit in Eddie's claim at all, since he "was an adult, lawfully detained in an adult jail" when he confessed and the Harling case was thus inapplicable because "the statement was not obtained by any use or misuse of juvenile court processes."

In oral argument, though, they had a bit of trouble explaining why it was all right to have questioned Harrison at the jail without first giving him a preliminary hearing. They could easily have taken him before a magistrate for that purpose before questioning him, and in fact they did that some days later. They had to admit, as the trial judge had said, that the procedure followed in Eddie's case maybe wasn't the best, but they didn't see that as reason enough to bar use of his confession.

It was a pretty lively argument, with the court proving less hostile than I had feared, and I came away feeling that we had a chance. One of the judges I had figured at the outset as a "conservative" had been much harder on the U.S Attorney in questioning than he had been on me, and while I knew that didn't necessarily mean anything, still, you never can tell. At least it seemed to me from the nature of his questions that he hadn't made up his mind yet, so there was hope. We needed only two votes and we just might get them.

When I got back to the office I wrote Eddie a letter. I couldn't go see him because he had been transferred from the D.C. Jail to the Federal Penitentiary at Lewisburg, Pennsylvania, but I knew he would be anxious to hear how things had gone. I ended the letter: "We have done all that we can for now and will simply have to wait for the court's opinion before we know whether anything further needs to be done." That was December 18, 1963. It was to be December 7, 1965, before we saw that opinion.

During the first eighteen months of that long wait we were completely in the dark as to what was going on. I checked at the clerk's office once in a while, to make sure the case wasn't just lost somewhere, although that couldn't happen. I just wanted to hear him say it wasn't and that there was nothing I could do to jar the decision loose. I felt as if I should be doing something—I'd never heard of the court sitting on a case so long. A few months, yes. It takes time to study a record thoroughly and write opinions. And this case had a lengthy, complex record. But a year and a half? How could they possibly take so long? What on earth were they doing?

Other cases came and went at the court, some of them on points similar to our confession point, some on speedy trial, some favorable and some unfavorable to our cause. Eddie would hear about them at Lewisburg and write asking about them. I saw him once during that period, at the D.C. Jail, when he was brought to Washington for a brief period to attend his mother's funeral. I never met her but George Thomas had, and told me she was a fine, respectable woman. A black kosher cook in a Jewish old folks home, he said. Eddie and I talked about the case and speculated about the outcome. He was discouraged by the delay but confident as ever that he would ultimately prevail.

I was beginning to doubt it very seriously. It wouldn't

take this long to reverse the conviction if that's what they were going to do. My thought was that they must be trying to uphold the conviction and were having a hard time doing it. Or maybe they were hopelessly divided on some point. I didn't know, and there was no way to find out and nothing to do but wait and see. It must have been maddening for Eddie.

Suddenly something happened. A telephone call from the clerk's office told me Eddie's case had been set for rehearing *en banc* on one question—the Harling point. There was to be no rehearing as to Sampson and White. It was June 2; the case was to be heard on June 15.

It couldn't have happened at a worse time for me. I already had an airline case set for argument *en banc* on that same day. It was the most important argument of my life up to that time, and I was up to my ears in work getting ready for it. I'd never had an *en banc* argument before and now I had two on the same day! I was stunned.

An *en banc* argument is relatively rare. What it means is that instead of being heard and and decided by a three-judge panel, the case is set for argument before all nine of the judges. The procedure is reserved for very important, controversial cases. A lawyer really wants to be on his toes and thoroughly prepared, because those nine judges can think up a lot of tough questions, and when you get them all together you'd better know what you're talking about and be ready to field any question imaginable. You can't possibly anticipate them all, but what you can do is read, read, read, and think, think, think, about every facet of your case. You're supposed to be the one person in the world who knows your case best, and you'd better be if you don't want to fall flat on your face. How could I get ready for two such cases at the same time? The court had sat on the case for a year and a half and then dumped it back on me at the one time I was most buried in other work that had to be done. Added to my travail was the fact that I was no longer able to command the armies of help that a big law firm can muster in emergencies. A few months before, I had left my former firm to go out on my own, with three younger partners.

I decided it didn't really matter that I was without assistants. An oral argument is an intensely personal thing, and it has to come from you, not somebody else. You could have somebody write you the prettiest speech in the world and it wouldn't do you any good when you got to court because those judges aren't the least bit interested in listening to you make a speech. After the first two sentences one of them will interrupt you with a question and that will be the end of your speech. You have to talk about what bothers them in the case if you have any hope of getting their vote.

By the time I had my nightcap that night I knew everything was going to be all right. From the Court of Appeals' action I could assume that we had lost the constitutional arguments on double jeopardy and speedy trial, as expected, and won on the confession arguments, also as expected, with one exception. The Harling point. I figured that the panel must have gone against us on that argument but that the liberals on the court wouldn't let the panel's opinion be issued and become the law without a battle. It was my understanding that before a panel's decision was publicly issued as an opinion of the court and became binding on all of the judges as a precedent to be followed in future cases, the opinion was circulated to all nine judges privately. This procedure gave the judges opportunity, if they wished, to try to keep a decision from becoming the law without the whole court's considering the matter in solemn conclave assembled. I wasn't sure that this was the procedure and I'm still not—maybe my guess was 100 percent wrong. But it made me feel confident that Eddie was going to win. Why would the court order rehearing *en banc* on the Harling question unless the panel had decided it adversely and a majority of the whole court felt the decision was wrong and should not become the law? That didn't have to be the reason for the court's ordering rehearing but it was likely reason, it seemed to me. Eddie's case was going to be a cake walk if I was right.

Anyway, the Supreme Court had recently issued an opinion that seemed to make Eddie's case foolproof. It was the Escobedo case which, together with a subsequent case on the same point, the Miranda case, evoked a storm of fury so strong that Congress later enacted a statute to reverse it. In the Escobedo case the court had reversed the conviction of a confessed murderer out in Illinois because the confession had been obtained before the prisoner had been given an opportunity to consult with his lawyer. The conservatives were outraged, not only because of the miscarriage of justice thus produced—freeing a confessed murderer—but because of the breadth of the new law announced by the case. The Mallory case had been bad enough, it was argued, but at least it applied only to federal cases, and did not intrude on states' rights. But the Escobedo decision did, in a big way. Whereas the Mallory decision was rested on federal rules of criminal procedure, which applied only to federal government prosecutions in federal courts, the Escobedo decision was rested on the Constitution of the United States, and applied to all criminal prosecutions in any court—federal, state, or local. It was one thing for the Supreme Court to say that Mallory's confession couldn't be used in a federal court in the District of Columbia, which was pretty much the bailiwick of the Supreme Court anyway. It was quite another thing for the Supreme Court to say that Escobedo's confession couldn't be used in a nonfederal case in Cook County, which was somebody else's bailiwick altogether. And where the Mallory case had been interpreted as allowing at least *some* police questioning of suspects before they were taken before a magistrate to be advised of their rights, Escobedo said the police couldn't question a suspect at all without letting him talk to his lawyer first. And as everybody knew, and the vigorously dissenting justices in the 5-to-4 Escobedo decision pointed out, any lawyer worth his salt would tell a suspect to clam up, with the result that there would be no confessions in criminal cases anymore and you could forget about making the world safe for democracy because we'd need the whole army right here to protect us against all the criminals who were going to run loose.

Of course it didn't turn out that way, and the Escobedo and Miranda decisions didn't seem to keep criminals from getting convicted every day, but they certainly eliminated any question of whether the police were beating up suspects to get confessions. But the whole question's up in the air again because Congress passed the Crime Control and Safe Streets Act of 1968, which contained a lot of good measures such as providing federal funds to assist local law enforcement efforts, but which also purported to overrule the Miranda, Escobedo, and Mallory decisions by giving the police permission to question suspects without a lawyer and before any preliminary hearing.

I say "purported" because Congress can't change the Constitution of the United States just by passing a law. It takes a constitutional amendment to do that. And when that new law gets used and some poor slob gets convicted by a confession that is permissible under the new law but not under the Miranda case decision, and his case gets up to the Supreme Court, who's going to decide whether he goes free or not and whether the new law is constitutional or not? Not Congress.

But Congress hadn't passed that law yet when Eddie's case was to be argued; the Escobedo case was the supreme law of the land without question under the "Warren Court," and Eddie had been questioned without being given an opportunity to consult with a lawyer, in violation of the Supreme Court's new holding. The Court of Appeals had pointedly ignored the Escobedo case in its order setting Eddie's case for rehearing *en banc,* directing me to address my argument to the Harling case. But they knew all about the Escobedo case, and I sure wasn't going to let them ignore it on June 15. There just wasn't any doubt about it in my mind—we were going to win going away, and after all that waiting Eddie was going to get out of jail.

The thing that really bothered me was the airline case. We were in trouble on that one for sure. We'd won the case before the panel, but the court had ordered rehearing *en banc.* That meant there was a better-than-even chance the court was getting ready to reverse the case, and that made me downright sick at the stomach. With a brand-new law firm, and out from under the protective umbrella of the big firm I had so recently left, I just couldn't lose the biggest aviation case in years. It involved the future of the whole airfreight industry; when we'd won it before the panel, the president of American Airlines, who was then Marion Sadler, had called me up to thank me personally for the victory, saying, "Al, I just don't know what we would have done if you hadn't won that case." It was a nice gesture, and even though I knew he was exaggerating the importance of the victory, I wasn't all that sure *he* knew it, and to lose the case at this point would be just awful.

At least I wouldn't be alone if it happened. Two of us were arguing the case on behalf of the major trunkline carriers, and had the last time around. The other lawyer was Warren Baker, resident Washington partner of a large Wall Street firm, and as fine a lawyer as you could find anywhere. But that was small comfort. This was a must-win case as far as I was concerned. A lot of important industry executives and lawyers would be there to hear the argument, including some from my own client, and I just had to be ready to do my best.

In that case, at least, I was in my own field. There need be no fear that the judges could think up too many questions I couldn't answer. This was my life at that time, arguing airline cases, and I loved it and knew the field like the palm of my hand. Better, in fact. But that wasn't enough to make me feel safe in the Court of Appeals. The airline field is a highly specialized, complex one. And, unlike the situation in a criminal case, the Court of Appeals was not expert on the subject. They were highly intelligent and sophisticated judges, but they were men, after all, and they couldn't possibly be experts on every subject; they might get one or two airline cases a year, if that. But their lack of familiarity with the subject matter could lead to all kinds of confusion in oral argument and I'd listened with horror one time while a judge, near the end of an argument, had asked a lawyer a question that revealed he'd missed the whole point of a lengthy, complicated argument because of a factual misunderstanding about the industry—a perfectly understandable thing, but frightening. So I always prepared for airline case oral arguments in court with some trepidation, taking special care to make sure I wasn't overlooking something that was common knowledge in the industry but unfamiliar to others and hence a source of possible disaster if not treated properly in court.

That process takes a lot of time and thought, and doesn't leave room for a similar effort at the same time on another case in an unfamiliar field. But that's the way it was, and there was nothing to do but get ready for both arguments as best I could and keep my fingers crossed.

To tell you the truth, the prospect pleased me after I got used to the impossible idea of having both cases up at the same time. It was really going to be fun. Easy things always bored me, difficulty challenged me, and the impossible was what I really liked to try my hand at. And way down deep I knew I could do both jobs with no great strain because I'd argued both cases before so the preparation job was mostly a matter of reviewing familiar territory. I was going to be busy for a couple of weeks, sure, but then think of the fun—two *en banc* arguments back-to-back on the same day, when most lawyers never get a chance to argue even one case *en banc* in a lifetime!

As it turned out, the cases were rescheduled, so they were argued on successive days rather than on the same day. Eddie's case came up first. There was one unpleasant surprise when the judges walked in. There were ten of them instead of nine. The most conservative of the judges on the panel that had heard Eddie's case the first time had "retired" the preceding October. But old circuit court judges, unlike old soldiers, don't even fade away, at least not right away. They become "senior circuit court judges," and as such continue to sit on cases when they feel like it. They don't have to work, because they get paid retirement money for life, but many of them do go on working, rendering a valuable service to the court above and beyond the call of duty. Our "retired" judge was there.

He had only one vote, but it was an important one. With a ten-judge court, Eddie needed six votes to win. With a nine-judge court he would have needed only five. And there was already one vote against him for sure, probably two, conceivably three, or we wouldn't be there for re-argument. But there had to be some strong support for our view of the case too, or we wouldn't be there. But that one judge's vote might make the difference by increasing the number of votes we needed to six. Damn! Why'd he have to come? He wouldn't be there tomorrow when I needed him for my airline case, I knew: he was sitting on this one only because he'd been on the original panel. But there he was today, big as life, and I expected him to do his best to protect the public from my "lad." Wouldn't you just know? Eddie was star-crossed, no two ways about it.

I began the argument with the traditional opening, "May it please the court." I fervently hoped it would! I briefly outlined the facts concerning Eddie's first confession. There were actually three confessions. First, Eddie had responded to oral questioning. Second, his oral statement had been reduced to writing on a typewriter and he had signed it. Third, he had given essentially the same statement to a prison official whose job it was to classify Eddie for internal jail purposes. This third confession was clearly inadmissible under prior Court of Appeals opinions, so we were not concerned with that. The second confession, in writing, was similarly inadmissible. We were concerned only with the first confession—Eddie's original statement to the police when first questioned at the jail. If that statement was admissible, you could forget the rest of the case because that statement said enough to convict him of first-degree murder. In it he admitted killing Brown, albeit accidentally, during an attempted robbery. So the name of the game was to find some reason why that statement was inadmissible, and the Court of Appeals had asked me to address myself to that question alone, directing my attention pointedly to the Harling case.

I addressed myself to the Harling case, as I had to, but in stating the facts I emphasized points having nothing to do with that case. I stressed facts showing how Eddie had been influenced in that initial interview by his lack of understanding of the felony murder rule—how he had been taken in and had confessed to an accidental killing, not realizing that he was confessing to first-degree murder—because he had not had the benefit of consulting a lawyer. I wasn't arguing just Harling, I was arguing Escobedo.

The court was strangely silent. I had expected a torrent of questions and comment. Instead I had an audience. I was puzzled, not knowing whether that was a good omen or bad. I went on talking to the quiet court, listening to my own words as if someone else were speaking them. I have often had that sensation in oral argument, as if someone else were arguing and I were a spectator, and the words were coming out of their own volition. It's as though I had two minds—one directing my mouth, while the other was standing by listening to the words only casually while surveying the judges, sensing the spectators, watching for reactions from opposing counsel, running through a thousand ideas like a drowning man is supposed to, searching, searching, searching, in a series of thoughts coming and going in almost instantaneous sequence. Sometimes I would find something, and I would intrude my thoughts on that independent mouth, to make a point it seemed to be missing. Sometimes I would hear it misspeak, and would correct it. But mostly I just let it run. I was familiar with its course, it spoke no surprises, it was well schooled on the case and knew what I wanted to say, or what I had thought the night before I wanted to say.

The voice went on, with only occasional interruption from the bench, until the end of my time was near. Then it began a closing argument I had planned in advance; my detachment was gone completely as I wholeheartedly joined my voice in a plea for the court not merely to reverse the convictions, which it seemed to me it had to and would, but to dismiss the case. With the confessions gone, the government would have no case against Eddie. The rest of the evidence fell far short of proving felony murder. But I was convinced that the U.S. Attorney's office would never dismiss the indictment against Eddie, whether they could make a case or not, as long as they had a legal excuse to keep him in jail. So I argued that it was far too late to afford Eddie the speedy trial guaranteed him and all citizens by the Sixth Amendment. It was now five years since Eddie had been charged with murder, and he had yet to be given a fair trial. Surely the constitutional requirement of a speedy trial demanded better performance by the judicial system than that. It was time and past to give meaning and effect to the constitutional command of a speedy trial. If those words could be stretched to encompass five years' delay, what meaning was left to them? I felt every word of that argument deeply. It wasn't Eddie who was on trial, it was a judicial system that could tolerate such a delay.

Chief Judge David Bazelon, sitting in the middle of the court, had his head bowed low, and was shaking it slowly and sadly. Nobody on the bench, not even the tenth judge, who had scowled through the rest of my argument, showed any trace of disagreement. I sat down in thunderous silence.

The rest was anti-climax. The U.S. Attorney made the expected noises, and I made some in rebuttal, emphasizing that his argument proved the point I had already made, that the U.S. Attorney's office was determined to keep Eddie in jail as long as possible whether they had any case or not. Further, they would not have a case if the court agreed that Eddie's confession was inadmissible and, accordingly, the court should not merely reverse the conviction but order dismissal of the indictment against Eddie because it was far too late to afford him a speedy trial. The Chief Judge expressed the thanks of the court for my services in this case, and for those of Mr. Thomas, who was beside me, and the judges left.

So much for Eddie, I thought. Tomorrow I had to argue the airline case, and there weren't many hours left for the last-minute preparations I needed. I was thinking about them before I got out of the courthouse. And, I thought, it would be just my luck to win Eddie's case, for which I got paid nothing, and lose the airline case, which was my bread and butter. And that's just what happened. The court upset Eddie's conviction 6 to 4. They upheld the Civil Aeronautics Board 6 to 3. I had never argued two cases any better in my life, and I don't think a word I said in the two days affected the outcome of either case in any way. Maybe I'm wrong. I'd like to think so in Eddie's case at least.

XIII

Same Old Story

(AI)

On December 7, 1965, the Court of Appeals handed down its opinion in the *en banc* hearing. They ruled out Eddie's oral confession on grounds of the Harling case. With the confessions gone, there was no evidence of felony murder left. I had visions of walking Eddie out of jail by Christmas.

The first step after the appeal was for the case to be returned to the District Court, where it had been tried originally. Several weeks later George Thomas phoned me and said that the formal presentment of the Court of Appeals decision would be in the assignment court on the following Thursday. He had been notified of that fact because he had been court-appointed counsel in the District Court at the prior trial. He said that there was no need for me to be there, but he assured me I was welcome to go along if I wished.

Wild horses couldn't have kept me away, as George well knew. For three years I'd been waiting for this day and I wanted to be there at the finish. But George told me he was

173

afraid I'd be disappointed. He didn't think anything much was going to happen that day. Eddie had not been brought back to the District from Lewisburg yet. White was in the Federal Penitentiary in Atlanta, and he didn't know where Sampson was. He thought the government would hold on to Eddie and the others as long as it could. That meant the government would go through all the motions of bringing the three to trial again, which would result in some delay.

I asked whether there was anything we could do to speed things up, to try to get the case dismissed. He said we could move for dismissal, and that he would ask for a speedy trial, but he doubted that these steps would be effective. I asked whether it would do any good for me to prepare a written motion, and he said it might, but again, he doubted it.

"I tell you, Al, I'm convinced they're going to keep those boys just as long as they can," he said. "They're not going to give up easily. No, indeed."

I went down to the assignment court, armed with a written motion for dismissal of the case. I'd never been in the assignment court before and I was amazed. The courtroom was jammed with people. On the spectators' side of a dividing rail the benches were full of witnesses and defendants. Inside the rail, at counsel tables and on benches and even in the jury box, were swarms of lawyers. Behind the high bench sat Chief Judge McGuire.

The clerk would call out a case name and number, and counsel in that case would respond, announcing that they were ready to go to trial or explaining why they were not. If both sides announced "ready," the Chief Judge would assign them to a judge and a courtroom, and off they would go to trial, followed by a group of the spectators. Before they could get out of the courtroom, the next case would be called and a new set of lawyers would respond.

The judge was brusque with U.S. Attorneys and defense counsel alike, bawling them out in a loud voice over the bustle of those coming and going. One U.S. Attorney explained that the government wasn't ready in a case where the defendant was prepared to go to trial.

"Why not? asked Judge McGuire in a tone that left no doubt he thought they should be.

The U.S. Attorney responded that he was not really familiar with the case and the then U.S. Attorney who had been handling the matter had gone out of town on vacation, not expecting the case to be called until the following week.

With obvious impatience the judge addressed the attorney by name and told him: "The government is never on vacation. That's no reason to hold up a case and I don't want it to happen again."

And so it went, with the judge granting or denying continuances to the seemingly endless parade of lawyers, while I waited with George Thomas. When the clerk called out *"United States* vs. *Eddie M. Harrison, Joseph R. Sampson, and Orson G. White,* Number 365–60," George stepped forward along with counsel for the other two prisoners. A U.S. Attorney stepped forward and said there could be no trial yet because the prisoners had not been brought back to the District of Columbia, but were in various prisons far away.

Judge McGuire wanted to know why. Here it was January and the case had been decided on December 7 and why hadn't the government gotten those men back here in a case as old as this one?

The U.S. Attorney apologized and attributed the failure to "administrative oversight."

"Administrative oversight, hell," I thought. I had personally called the U.S. Attorney's office a month before to make sure he knew where the prisoners were and would take the necessary steps to get them here, and I had been assured that this would be done.

George spoke up with a motion to dismiss the case for lack of prosecution.

"Denied," said the judge.

175

George invited the judge's attention to our motion for dismissal that had been filed. The judge hadn't seen it. George handed a copy up to him. It was several pages long and he didn't read past the first few words.

"Speedy trial," he said; "haven't these defendants already been tried and convicted twice before? If you ask me, they're lucky to be getting another trial at all. I'll deny your motion."

He set the case for February.

When our day came up we went down to the assignment court again. This time the government couldn't proceed because they'd discovered that a key witness, Valentine, was in the army and was serving overseas. How much time would it take to get him back? The government wasn't sure, but they would take the necessary steps to find out, and to secure Valentine's return. George moved for dismissal for lack of prosecution but was summarily overruled.

There was nothing we could do but wait. Sooner or later they'd run out of excuses and have to let Eddie go because they had no case. But not soon. The trial was eventually set for May 2.

On that day George and I went to court prepared to "walk our man out." The government was going through the motions of going to trial, but we knew that they couldn't prove felony murder without the confessions that the Court of Appeals had thrown out of the case. By the end of the day Eddie would be free at last.

Jury selection was almost perfunctory, and the Assistant U.S. Attorney started to put on his witnesses. Poor guy, he hardly had any, and what they had to say didn't amount to much. They could prove Brown was dead, and that Eddie had admitted the killing to Valentine, the witness returned from the wars for the trial, but they couldn't prove that the killing had occurred during the course of an attempted robbery. That was essential to their case because Eddie was being tried under a one-count indictment charging no other offense. He had to be found guilty of felony murder or nothing.

Before the morning was over, the government's evidence was all in. Then the Assistant U.S. Attorney turned to the judge and calmly announced: "At this time I would like to read the testimony of defendants White and Harrison which was made at the last trial."

The judge said, "Very well."

I couldn't believe my ears.

George Thomas was actually trying the case, and I was at the counsel table with him only as an assistant to him, and I couldn't really even assist him because he was an expert trial lawyer and I'd never even attended a criminal trial as a spectator before, let alone as a lawyer. I was just there to listen and to watch Eddie walk out of court a free man. And there were experienced defense counsel there representing Orson White and Joseph Sampson. It was my place to sit still and shut up, but when that judge said "Very well," I just couldn't resist:

"Your Honor, we object to the reading of the testimony," I said.

If they read that testimony we were in big trouble. At the previous trials Eddie had taken the witness stand and practically repeated the whole story told in the confessions that we had worked so long and hard to have ruled inadmissible. At those prior trials he'd had no choice. With the confessions in evidence, he had to go on the stand and explain them away or be convicted.

But Eddie's story was about as damaging as the confessions. The only difference was that Eddie claimed he'd gone to Brown's door to pawn a shotgun that he didn't know was loaded—and who would ever believe that? Two juries hadn't; this one wouldn't either; and if the judge let the prosecutor read that old testimony out of the transcript, Eddie's chances were just about zero—they might as well read the confessions.

177

The judge turned me off fast: "You don't represent White."

Of course I didn't. I shut up. But I was stunned. The handwriting was on the wall. When they finished reading White's testimony they were going to read Eddie's, and George could object all he wanted to but the judge was going to overrule him.

And that's just what happened. They read Eddie's damaging testimony.

XIV

Guilty as Charged

(*Eddie*)

It is not so dramatic when a man is actually sentenced to life imprisonment; the drama is in those closing minutes before the verdict. That's when a man has to fight; that's when he's prepared to shout for joy, scream out to the Lord for mercy, or close the doors to his protective shell and do neither.

Will the defendant stand and face the jury—? It takes a long time to stand, hands on the table. You slowly rise and look at the juror sitting on the end next to the judge's bench. He's the foreman. They all look toward you and you look back; you have to—you are compelled to. They have something that you want so badly, clues—look closer, do they look happy, sad, is anyone's head down, the women, are there any tears, smiles, the eyes, look at the eyes! Panic—I can't find their eyes, they won't let me look into their eyes—Oh My God! I can't find their eyes. The foreman is standing; he's looking at a piece of paper in his hand—

"Mr. Foreman, how do you find the defendant Eddie M. Harrison?"

Two seconds is about all the time you have to prepare for the most important decision of your life. Two seconds —a hell of a long time. The breaking point, the fine line between life and death.

The foreman is reading from his piece of paper: "We find the defendant, Eddie M. Harrison, guilty as charged!"

Now I see the eyes, now they want to see my eyes. There is nothing to see; the door has closed, the shell is intact, I don't feel the pain, "My head is bloody, but unbowed." It's just another setback. We'll win—it only means a few more years. My mother can't cry for me now and it doesn't hurt as much. I'm spared the extra pain of her burden.

Al Prather is crushed; he bleeds for me, but he shouldn't. I can take it. I've learned how to wait. "The agony of the years finds me and shall find me, unafraid." We'll win, I know we will, we must!

We're back on the legal road again. Appeal, appeal, to someone, to something. I couldn't face Lewisburg again, the pity of fellow inmates was something I neither wanted nor desired.

I elected not to serve the sentence, which meant that the time spent from that day on would not count. It also meant that I couldn't be transferred out of the jurisdiction.

The D.C. Jail had changed in a lot of ways. There had been an administrative turnover; several of the black privates I knew were now lieutenants, and one was even a captain. Even the superintendent of the jail was black. There really had been some changes made. The metal benches had been replaced by tables and chairs in the dining rooms and there were even a television set and Ping-Pong tables in the dining room. Inmates were permitted to stay out of their cells until eleven o'clock and could write to whomever they chose.

I was treated as somewhat of a dignitary when I returned to the jail. It was nice to be home!

Cell Block 3 was an honor cell block of sorts. The men there were all on work details throughout the jail. I was transferred there as cell block clerk shortly after my return. All of the men in CB 3 had special privileges. Since nearly all of them were serving time, an attempt was made to provide special programs for them.

I began to get actively involved in the jail programs. I became a recreation aide, planning recreational activities for the rest of the inmates.

Maurice Lewis was my supervisor. Maurice had grown up in old Georgetown and had played a lot of sports and worked with young kids in the community. He eventually found himself working as a guard in the D.C. Jail. The jail had created the position of Recreation Supervisor and Maurice had been selected. I was his staff. We often talked of what a good recreation program should look like. Some of my ideas were a little too far out for Maurice. He had to consider what the jail would let him do and I was mostly concerned with what should be done.

We were able to reconcile our different interests and come up with some very substantial programs. In trying to create activities to take the boredom and frustration out of being in jail for the whole population, I had found a solution to my own needs. Nothing is more therapeutic than helping someone else. Soon the jail became alive with recreational activities—intramural baseball and basketball teams, talent shows, card tournaments, special dinners for inmate birthdays, Christmas shows, an inmate band—anything we could get away with.

My role as an inmate was lost completely. I was viewed by many as a staff member. I had a certain power to influence some of the things that were being done and it didn't matter that I didn't get credit for it as long as it was done.

New York Reds was serving twelve years for a narcotic

violation; he was the jail printer and we both worked out of the administrative offices at the jail. Reds had the distinction of having been confined in the jail longer than anyone else. He was probably the most influential inmate there. We became partners. Reds knew how to "jail"—we often sought each other's advice when we were going to make any kind of move. He had about ten or twelve guards in his hip pocket and was very careful and cautious. I didn't have his kind of refinement; as a matter of fact, I was pretty reckless at times and probably caused Reds some of his gray hairs. I was never concerned with methods, only that things were done. When he found out that I was sending memos to the cell block officers telling them to extend the recreation period, he nearly flipped. Reds constantly reminded me that I was an inmate and couldn't do things like that!

The greatest recreational need at the jail was difficult to provide, but Reds and I worked on it. WOMEN! There had to be some way to get to the women. There was a Women's Division just a hundred feet away and I was sure we could talk somebody into letting a group of the men go over there.

I wrote a memo giving the jail band authority to play at the Women's Division and relying on the fact that the Associate Superintendent wouldn't read it. I typed a little line at the bottom with the word "Approved" and a place for his signature. He signed it. The band practiced like hell for the next couple of days. It was soon a standing rule for the jail band to play at the Women's Division whenever there was a show put on for the other cell blocks.

Maurice Lewis and I had talked about the possibility of getting free tickets to the Washington Senators' baseball games and taking some of the inmates out of the jail to attend. He felt there would be problems but decided it was at least worth a try. A number of the officers would volunteer their time if we could come up with the tickets. The tickets were easy enough; who in the hell pays to watch the Washington Senators, anyway? It was a very good idea and Maurice was able to sell it to the Superintendent. There was one big problem, though: how to select the inmates to go. That was left up to Reds and me. One escape could ruin the whole program. Reds and I both knew most of the guys who would leap at an opportunity to be outside the walls unguarded, and we also knew the ones who would benefit from a few hours of freedom and return. It was very exciting to discuss all the possibilities. We could have gotten rich by selling "escape passes."

After five or six games, Maurice and I talked about my going to one of the baseball games. The program had been very successful, and he knew that I had done a hell of a lot to help screen out anyone who would jeopardize it. I had never given it much thought; it was unheard of to let a convicted murderer go to a ball game with unarmed guards. Hell, he was game, so why not? There were some problems, but no one seriously doubted that I would return. I had no intention at all of trying to escape. Too many people had invested too much in me to do something as foolish as that. How could I ever betray the faith that Al Prather had in me?

I was permitted to go to the ball game and had one hell of a time. There was one moment of near panic. I had to go to the bathroom and was expecting to be escorted.

"Hey, Maurice, I gotta go piss, man."

"Go ahead. It's down the ramp somewhere."

I got up and left the stands; I was deliriously happy and almost overwhelmed with the thought of being totally free for the first time in more than six years. As I passed people in the corridor I was somehow expecting them to stare at me. Didn't they know what this represented? I had the biggest, widest grin on my face that I've ever worn. I wanted to skip, wave my arms in the air, and twirl around and around. I was crazy with joy. Walking down the long corridor, I felt a sudden urge to just run away. There were thousands of people going in all directions; there was no way for anyone to stop me; it was all my decision. I had a choice between returning to face the courts again, where there had not been any justice, or taking my freedom. It felt so good to be free, away from the jail, guards, courts, pressure, doubt, lonely nights. . . . STOP IT, WHAT AM I DOING? I don't want to think these thoughts; where did they come from? I only want to go to the bathroom. Where is the bathroom? How long have I been gone? Are they looking for me? Maybe they think I'm trying to escape? I have to get back. I wasn't watching the direction I was going in, so I wasn't really sure how to get back. I walked fast in the opposite direction, almost panicking when I realized that I didn't even know the section we were sitting in. I remembered the view of the field was from the third base line and I headed in that direction. I had absolutely no idea of how long I had been gone and I almost fought my way through the crowd.

"Hey, Eddie, we ordered you a coke while you were gone. Did you find the john all right?"

"Yeah, I found it!" How silly of me to lie about it, but how could I tell the truth? I still had to go to the bathroom, but I was determined to wait it out. The last thing I wanted was a damn coke!

A lot of people were relieved when I returned to the jail; some didn't believe that I had actually come back. It was an unheard of practice to begin with.

After the third trial was over, I didn't feel that I had a lot of time to waste feeling sorry for myself or being bitter. My life in jail had some meaning—I was really getting involved in things. The need for change was readily apparent and I could actually see where I was having some impact. It was strange to try and relay these feelings to Al. We both had our sights set on my being turned loose, and although the last conviction had been a crushing blow, it didn't dampen my spirits or desire to continue the fight. Al had his cause to fight and I had mine: we fought on different battlefields, but our commitments were equal. I was determined to make the jail a more humane place to live in and Al was determined to have me free.

Among his other jobs, New York Reds was also editor of the jail magazine. I began to write feature articles—commenting on current events, reporting what was happening around the jail, explaining legal opinions and their effect. We broadened the mailing list for the *Insider* and began to send copies to civic groups, colleges, employers, judges. We also solicited outside groups to come to the jail and speak to the evening inmate discussion groups.

A lot of these discussion group topics centered around crime. It seemed like people would always expect the inmate participants to have the answers to these problems and I guess we should have. The jail could easily have been called the "Crime Preparation Institute," because inmates did in fact prepare there to continue a life of crime—but why not? Most of them would never get a fair chance when released, nor would they be able to care for themselves or their families. There wouldn't be anything left but a life of crime, so why not take the only option open?

A lot of people were frightened after these discussion groups because the myth of prison rehabilitation was always shattered and there was never a happy ending to the story.

XV

Third Appeal

(Al)

I went to see Eddie in jail expecting him to be demoralized. He wasn't. I don't mean he was happy or anything like it, but he hadn't lost hope and he wasn't blaming anybody. In fact, before I left he was trying to cheer me up. He had faith in his case and faith in his lawyer and faith that we would win ultimately no matter what, and he could wait again—as he had so long already. I told him we should win the appeal but there were no guarantees. We could get another tough bench and lose as we had before; there was no way of knowing whether I was right on the law.

"You're right," he said. "You've *got* to be!"

So I set out to be. I talked to George Thomas about the appeal. There were just two appellants left, Eddie and Orson White. Sampson had been acquitted by the judge at the trial because there was no damaging testimony from prior trials to read against him. So now there were two left in jail and one back out on the street. It was the summer of 1966,

186

three years after I'd first been appointed to the case and had first turned to George Thomas for help.

I turned to George again, and found him as responsive and willing to help as ever. He was determined to see this thing through. He believed in Eddie Harrison and thought the decision was all wrong. He criticized himself needlessly and unfairly for having failed to persuade the jury to let Eddie go. We asked the court to appoint us both—one to represent Eddie and one to represent Orson—so that there would be no unnecessary delay in the appeal. A new lawyer appointed for Orson would have to waste a lot of time familiarizing himself with the record. Already this case was so long and complex as almost to defy comprehension.

We hit the books. There were three obvious points to argue: first, the use of the earlier testimony. That was our gut argument, the one we really had to win to get anywhere. Then there was our old "speedy trial" argument that we'd lost before—after all, the case wasn't getting any younger. And there was a third argument—that all three defendants should have been acquitted when Sampson was because there was insufficient evidence to prove attempted robbery, an essential element of the crime of felony murder.

It didn't take long to write the brief because the case we had was simple—frighteningly so. We had no great chance on the second two points, and the first one was an argument that had to be won on the basis of the judges' instincts—their sense of fairness and views of proper judicial procedure. And those are subjects you don't persuade judges about much. That's where they live. The most a lawyer can do with a case like that is serve it up in the way most likely to catch the conscience of the court—and keep his fingers crossed that he will get a liberal bench.

The argument was bottomed on the Fifth Amendment—the part of it all the crooks hide behind in court and before congressional committees: "No person shall be . . . compelled in any criminal case to be a witness against himself."

A lot of people want to do away with that these days because it causes a lot of trouble in pinning a crook down and putting him in jail. The Inquisition was much quicker. A little too quick for a lot of innocent people who got killed by it. And so was a lot of other quick justice that depended on forcing a man to testify against himself in merry old England. They put an end to it over there and we copied them in the Bill of Rights. That's how the Fifth Amendment got started in the first place.

Of course there was a little problem with arguing the Fifth Amendment in Eddie's case. Nobody had forced him to testify, and in fact he hadn't testified. They had just read his testimony from a former trial. And reading someone's testimony from a former trial is perfectly acceptable procedure in the usual case.

But this wasn't the usual sort of case. The testimony Eddie had given at the former trial wasn't exactly voluntary. When the confessions had been put in evidence at that trial, Eddie really had no choice but to go on the stand and tell his side of the story. Otherwise he was going to be convicted for sure. When those confessions were thrown out and Eddie got a new trial, he could safely refuse to take the stand and he did. But they put him on the stand without his ever leaving the defense table when they read his old testimony. They had made him the chief witness against himself at this trial and convicted him out of his own mouth with testimony given before, only because he had to give it to rebut the illegal confessions.

Didn't it mean anything when the Court of Appeals had thrown out the confessions? If Eddie was entitled to a new trial, shouldn't it be a fair one in which his constitutional privilege not to be a witness against himself was honored? What kind of Alice-in-Wonderland court system did we have if it took the judges of the Court of Appeals two years to decide a case that was absolutely meaningless because it had no practical effect?

The problem of persuading the court that this result should not prevail was simplified by another rule the Supreme Court had announced long before. That was the so-called "fruit of the poisonous tree" doctrine. It had grown up in a series of cases where the government had used illegal telephone wiretaps to obtain information to be used in prosecutions. It was against the law to intercept telephone messages, and when wires were nevertheless tapped, the intercepted messages could not be used as evidence in court. But how about the evidence the police discovered by following up on information obtained by an illegal wiretap? The Supreme Court had decided that such evidence was "tainted" by the original illegal wiretap and couldn't be used as evidence. It was dubbed "fruit of the poisonous tree" in one of the first cases on the subject, and the label stuck. The rule didn't apply just to illegal wiretaps.

So how about Eddie's case? His testimony at the first two trials had been obtained only by the prosecutor's using illegal confessions. Didn't that make Eddie's testimony "fruit" of this illegal action? We argued that it did; hence the trial judge never should have let the prosecutor read the old testimony to the jury at the trial.

The government brief pooh-poohed this argument and said we couldn't cite a single case to support our argument. They were right about that. We couldn't find a single case where a defendant's testimony from a former trial had been held inadmissible in a second one on the theory we were urging. And we'd done an awful lot of research looking for a case like that.

I say we. Really the guy who did most of the looking was a bright young Harvard lawyer named Roger Craig, who had come to work as an associate in our firm. He'd spent hours poring over the law books looking for a case like ours and there just weren't any to be found.

I didn't really care. It was as obvious as the nose on your

face that the government couldn't get away with such a rotten trick. If the government couldn't use the confessions because they were illegally obtained, they couldn't use the "fruit" of those confessions. We had to win, that's all there was to it.

I went to the oral argument full of confidence in our case. When the judges came out, I wasn't too happy with the panel we had drawn, but then I wasn't really unhappy with it either. They weren't exactly what you'd call bleeding hearts, but they weren't the toughest judges for a criminal case either. It seemed to me that we should be able to win with them.

George Thomas and I both argued—he for White and I for Eddie. We had a joint brief for the two appellants and had divided up the argument beforehand. It went pretty well, I thought, though you couldn't really tell from the questions which way the court might be heading.

One point drew fire—but not from the bench. I had closed the rebuttal argument with an impassioned plea for the court to dismiss the indictment against Eddie for lack of a speedy trial. I know Fourth of July oratory is for juries, not the Court of Appeals, but I can't help it. When I get wound up with something I feel strongly about, I just have to hammer it home. Maybe it's because my father and grandfather were both preachers and it's just in my blood. Anyway, I made a pretty strong speech and said that I was convinced the government would keep the prisoners in jail as long as they could, whether they had a real case or not. I meant it then and I still believe it, and I'm not one bit sorry I made such a fuss about it.

But the U.S. Attorney was mad as a wet hen. Not the one who actually argued the case. He and I shook hands in a friendly enough fashion after the judges left. But as I turned to leave, his boss came up to me with blazing eyes and accused me of casting wrongful aspersions on the honor of the U.S. Attorney's office. I shrugged him off and

went with a couple of my partners to Paul Young's great
restaurant for the soothing ministrations of my favorite
captain, Louie, and my reward of two martinis with lunch
and the inevitable post mortem of the argument. I thought
no more about the U.S. Attorney's remark until a few days
later when I received a letter from him.

United States Department of Justice
Office of the United States Attorney
Washington, D.C. 20001

November 16, 1966

Alfred V. J. Prather, Esquire
1707 L Street, N.W.
Washington, D.C. 20036

Re: *Harrison & White* v. *United States*
    USCA Nos. 20280 and 20281

Dear Mr. Prather:

It was with considerable regret that I witnessed during your oral
argument this morning the accusation that the Government, in bad faith,
had and would, if given an opportunity in the future, proceed to try
appellants knowing it had insufficient evidence, solely for the purpose
of "keeping these men in jail." It was certainly inappropriate and
beneath the calling of court-appointed counsel to fall upon such a term
as "a farce and mockery," in characterizing the proceedings had or
possibly to be had against the appellants. While ordinarily I might be
constrained to view such an attack on the Office of the United States
Attorney as the product of misguided zeal or loss of objectivity by counsel in the heat of the moment, in this instance it is quite apparent that
your words, though wholly irrelevant, were coldly calculated. It would
seem that your unwarranted comment also criticized the Courts of this
jurisdiction for sanctioning any proceedings subsequent to the indictment in this murder case when, particularly after the first trial the extent
of the prosecution's evidence was well known.

On behalf of this office and its two previous chief incumbents who have
participated in previous trials, I respectfully submit an apology is due
from you. See Canon 17 of the Canons of Professional Ethics of the
American Bar Association.

191

I shall not, at this time, send copies of this letter to the members of the hearing division without your consent.

Sincerely,
/s/
Assistant United States Attorney

Ain't that sumpthin'? You knock yourself out for free and what do you get? Threats from the government. I didn't bother to answer the letter. I couldn't top anything that funny.

The day after the argument I went down to the jail to see Eddie. He was glad to see me, as always, and anxious for news of how things had gone in court. We kicked the thing around until he had exhausted all possible inquiries. I ended that subject on an optimistic note and we turned to talking about his hopes for the future.

He was as sure as ever that he'd be out before long. He was working in the prison recreation program. He told me about some of their activities, and I was surprised to find he had a talent he'd never mentioned before. He was guitarist in the inmates' band, and they'd played for a dance attended by inmates of the women's reformatory. He also was studying to complete his high school education. They'd had a banquet attended by Judge Fauntleroy of the Juvenile Court, and Eddie had sat next to him and bent his ear about his case. The judge was interested, Eddie said, and I might be hearing from him about a jurisdictional point Eddie and I had never thought about. Eddie had written letters to some city officials concerning some ideas he had about juvenile rehabilitation. Hell, he was more active *inside* jail than most people are on the *outside*. I wondered what he'd do when he got out. And I wondered whether he would. I had to believe he would, because his faith was too strong not to be infectious.

The Court of Appeals wasn't infected, though. They

192

voted us down 3 to 0. The opinion was written by the only
black judge on our Court of Appeals, and it was his first
opinion since he'd been promoted to that court from the
District Court. He agreed with the government that we
couldn't support our argument with a single case. It was
a jim-dandy opinion, knocking down every one of our arguments very carefully, and I thought it was the dumbest
thing I'd ever read. Or at least the dumbest since the last
case I'd lost, because I always think court opinions against
my case are stupid. I know guys who can accept court decisions against their clients without blinking an eye and read
the opinions as dispassionately as if they'd had nothing to
do with the case, but I'm not built that way. I *hate* to lose
a case and I hate the piece of paper that says I lost, and
I don't care if that paper contains the nicest piece of legal
reasoning and writing you ever saw. I think it's dumb,
dumb, dumb, from beginning to end!

This one was especially dumb because it was the unani-
mous opinion of the three judges. You'd think at least *one*
of them would have had enough sense to see it our way and
write a dissent, but no. We had to lose it 3 and 0. And this
was the case I'd told Eddie we ought to win. Beautiful!

I went down to the jail to break the bad news to Eddie.
He knew about the decision before I got there. He was
more despondent than I'd ever seen him. I didn't know
what to say to cheer him up and I didn't know any reason
for him to be cheerful. He'd been sweating this thing out
a long time. We'd had high hopes—and now this!

We talked about what we could do next. For one thing,
we could petition for rehearing *en banc*. And if that didn't
work, we could try to go to the Supreme Court. But those
were both long shots, and Eddie knew it as well as I did.
The plain fact of the matter was that we'd just had our best
chance and lost it in a big way. It hurt and you could see
the hurt in Eddie's eyes. He wasn't all broken up or anything, just quiet and serious. I tried to be hopeful about

the next step in the case, but I was whistling in the dark and we both knew it.

When I was ready to leave, Eddie shook my hand the way he always does—a two-handed shake with his left hand lightly grasping my forearm—and looked at me with steady dark eyes. "I know you'll do all you can," he said. "Don't worry about me; I can stand it however it comes out." He headed back to the cell block door with firm steps, his back as straight as ever.

I went back to the office and stared blankly out the window above the people scurrying across the intersection of Connecticut Avenue and L Street. I felt about the same way I did the day they brought President Kennedy past that same corner on the way to St. Matthew's for the requiem mass. Only I hadn't killed President Kennedy. I could hate somebody else for that. But who could I hate for Eddie's wasted life? Who had just condemned him to a life sentence by being a bum lawyer and losing a case that should have been won? You think professional detachment keeps a lawyer from blaming himself for something like that? Maybe it does for some. But I wouldn't want them to represent me.

XVI

Big Court, Big Decision

(AI)

Roger Craig burst into my office excitedly. "I've found it! There's a line of California cases exactly on point, supporting our argument right down the line. And the key opinion is by Traynor. There's a new volume of the Decennial Digest and I was checking it out on the same headings I'd used before and there it was—not just one case but a whole line. I looked them up and they're perfect."

I couldn't believe my ears. The decision against Eddie had rested heavily on the fact that exhaustive research by the lawyers on both sides plus the court itself had failed to reveal any precedent for our contention—and now Roger had turned it up.

I went to the library to read the cases myself. Roger was right. These cases said that we should have won our case— that Eddie's old testimony should not have been used against him at the retrial.

There was only one hitch. These were decisions of a California court, not the District of Columbia court, so they weren't actually binding on our court. That's one of the many peculiarities in the law stemming from our state-federal division of government. The Supreme Court of a state can decide the law means one thing and a federal court can decide it means just the opposite, and unless the case involves certain kinds of questions where federal law overrides state law, even the Supreme Court of the United States can't do anything about it. So finding those cases would have set Eddie free in California, but not necessarily in the District of Columbia.

If we'd found these cases in time for our original brief and argument, our court would probably have followed them. The Supreme Court of California is an excellent one, and Chief Justice Traynor's views commanded respect from other judges. But now the problem was tough because our court had already decided the case the other way. They couldn't just follow Traynor's lead now, but had to decide that he was right and they were wrong.

The best way for us to go after that kind of a decision was to ask for a rehearing *en banc* so that we would have a shot at all nine of the judges on our court, not just the three who'd already voted against us; there would be at least six judges sitting who could follow Traynor without reversing themselves, and we needed only five to win.

We filed a petition for rehearing *en banc* relying on the California cases, and I went down to the jail to see Eddie and talk to him about it. He was pleased with our paper and the new cases. And he had some papers of his own to show me—some more writing on his ideas about juvenile rehabilitation programs. He actually seemed more inter-ested in these ideas for keeping other people out of the mess he was in than he was in his own case. It was good to see him in better spirits.

When I went to see him some time later, though, it was back to the blues again. The court had turned down our petition for rehearing *en banc* without even letting us argue the case orally. There was no opinion, just a flat denial. But there was one ray of hope. Chief Judge Bazelon, joined by Judge McGowan, had written a dissenting opinion—a nice, succinct statement of what was wrong with the decision, with a footnote citing our California cases. That dissent gave us a big step toward our only remaining chance, which was a petition for certiorari to the Supreme Court.

That was a mighty slim chance. The Supreme Court doesn't take many criminal cases. If you lose in the Court of Appeals in a federal criminal case, that's usually the end of the line, because the *right* to appeal ends in that court. Further appeal to the Supreme Court is a matter of *grace*, not right. You ask the court to consider your case in a piece of paper called a petition for certiorari. But the court's time is limited. It gets about 3,000 petitions for certiorari every year, and about 100 or 150 of them are granted, so the chances of getting to the Supreme Court are about thirty to one. In criminal cases the odds are even worse—about fifty to one.

Not very good odds, but they were all we had and that's what I told Eddie. I also told him, though, that we had a lot better chance than average of getting the Supreme Court to hear our case because it was more interesting from a legal standpoint than most. And we had the advantage of having on our side two of the most respected chief judges in the land—Traynor and Bazelon. That was bound to make somebody up there think twice about our case. Hopefully four somebodies, because that's how many votes it takes to get certiorari. They pass all those thousands of petitions around among the nine justices, and if four of them vote to hear the case, your petition is granted.

Ours was. And I wasn't the least bit surprised. By the time I'd finished the petition for certiorari I was so sold on our chances of getting the Court to hear our case that I would have been surprised if they hadn't. Partly that was just the reasoning of a lawyer selling himself on his own case. That's a bad habit shared by most lawyers and almost all clients. You get so wrapped up in your own cause that you lose perspective. But my belief in Eddie's case was more than that. You know how you feel once in a while that something's just *got* to happen? More a hunch than just wishful thinking? I had been feeling that way about Eddie's case for some time.

I went to the jail with the good news. Eddie was elated. His luck had finally turned. It was December, 1967. Eddie had been in jail now for almost seven years. He'd had his hopes dashed so many times you'd think he'd have given up long since, but he hadn't. And now, after his darkest hours facing his longest chances, he'd won the big one—a hearing in the Supreme Court. It wasn't victory yet by any means; the case wasn't won, it was just going to be heard. But the odds looked like nothing compared to what they had been. The chances of getting certiorari were against you, but the chances of winning *if* you got certiorari were about fifty-fifty. Eddie and I both left the rotunda with new bounce in our step.

I was a lot less bouncy three months later as I climbed the great flight of steps to the entrance of the Supreme Court. I'd been up those steps a lot of times, but never to argue a case there myself, and that made a big difference. I was scared. I'm always nervous before an oral argument, even one before a familiar tribunal where I'm arguing subjects I know well. It's a good thing, really, because it gets the old adrenalin running and sharpens the wits for the argument. It's the same as stage fright and leaves as soon as I get on my feet and start speaking. But sometimes it's pretty bad before an argument and today it was awful.

If you've ever been there, you know the Supreme Court is a pretty imposing place. After climbing a mountain of marble steps you enter through huge white columns into a great, high-vaulted hallway. It is usually lined with tourists waiting to go in to see a few minutes of the Court's proceedings. At the end of the hallway are two doors obviously intended for giants to enter. At the doors guards make sure you don't carry anything that might be dangerous into the courtroom itself. I remember how important I felt my first year out of law school carrying a big briefcase past those guards. One of them asked if I was carrying it as counsel in a case there, which I was (as an assistant to my boss, who was arguing a big case), and I said yes and marched right on past the tourist lines into the courtroom just like a big shot.

I did the same thing now, and I was legitimately in the big time, but I sure didn't feel like any big shot. I just felt sick in my stomach and weak-kneed.

The Court had not yet convened when I entered, so I looked around as I always do in any courtroom. The Supreme Court sits in a large room with an impressively high ceiling, huge columns along the side, and great long velvet draperies. About half the room is filled with spectator benches. A rail separates them from the chairs and tables for counsel, the lectern in front of the long bench where the justices sit, and places for court officials, law clerks, news reporters, and special visitors privileged to sit up front. Behind the justices' bench are more of those huge columns and the draperies from which the justices emerge in their black robes when the clerk intones his "Oyez, oyez, oyez" at the appointed hour for the Court's sessions.

Before that happens, there's a little bustle, with everybody getting into place and messenger boys in black knickers and long socks putting books and papers on the bench in front of the justices' chairs or bringing in water pitchers and tending to other homely chores. And when the Court comes in it's almost all anti-climax because they just stroll in talking and laughing, informal as you please, like any group of men on their way to work. They look around the courtroom and nod to people and lean over to talk to each other at the bench and in general give the impression that you're in a pretty informal, friendly place and not being thrown to the lions at all.

Of course you know damn well you *are* being thrown to the lions, because those nice friendly guys up there are Supreme Court justices and they are there to take your case apart at the seams and ask you embarrassing questions and snort at you and maybe fuss at you or laugh at you when you say something they disagree with. I've seen them really put lawyers down hard more than once, and it's no fair at all because there are nine of them picking on one guy and they have all the cards!

All but one. You're the one person in the room who really knows your case. They've read the opinion of the court below and the briefs, and a certain amount of the record, so they know a lot about your case—and they know the law and they have vast experience. But you're the real expert on the facts and the record, and that's why you're there. They want to ask you questions about that record. They want to explore your ideas and see whether you've brought them a problem they really ought to do something about, or whether they should just leave things the way the lower court decided.

Eddie's story interested them. They made it plain they thought he was guilty. At least Mr. Justice Marshall did. At one point in the argument he interrupted to say, "So he pointed a loaded shotgun at the man's head and just 'accidentally' blew it off, did he?"

That was bad news. Mr. Justice Marshall was the only black man on the Court, a liberal who'd written strong opinions I thought were favorable to our case, and as a private attorney he had successfully appealed some great civil liberty confession cases. I had really expected him to be focusing on the illegality of the confessions and the impropriety of using them against this poor helpless defendant who'd been held in jail illegally so long—and here he was picking on Eddie instead.

However, I was pleased with a question that followed shortly from Mr. Justice Harlan. He was the author of a recent opinion that I thought strongly favored our argument, and he asked me what that case meant to ours. I disclaimed any intention of telling him what that particular opinion meant, which brought a chuckle or two from other justices who had seen more than one lawyer try to tell a justice what his own opinion meant. However, in response to further questioning I suggested that I thought the other case indicated that Eddie should win his.

I turned to arguing Eddie's old "speedy trial" point, and when I started fussing about the Court of Appeals' taking two years to make a decision, the whole Court seemed to burst into activity. Mr. Chief Justice Warren just looked straight ahead gravely, but the four on each side of him were all turning to each other, making private comments, with much grinning and head-shaking. I didn't know whether they were making fun of the Court of Appeals or me, but I was sure they got the point and that was the main thing.

The day after the argument I drove down to the D.C. Jail to see Eddie. It was April 5, 1968, the day after the assassination of Dr. Martin Luther King. Rioting had broken out in Washington the night before. I seemed to be the only white moving on the streets through the ghetto. Broken windows and charred store fronts could be seen everywhere. The radio tensely reported rumors of additional trouble to come. I wondered whether there had been trouble at the jail—whether I would be able to get in—whether I would get there safely. I thought about my son David, a choir boy at the National Cathedral, where Dr. King had spoken on the previous Sunday. David had sat near Dr. King during the service, remembered his message vividly, and was broken up and angry over his death, which had pushed the memory of yesterday's Supreme Court argument out of family conversation. The whole world seemed strangely out of focus. It was a mad world, full of senseless violence and hate and fear. A sense of frustration and foreboding pervaded the very air. The breath of spring had lost its usual promise of beauty and resurrection—lost it in man's promises of smoke and fire and tear gas and destruction and every hateful emotion Dr. King had fought against.

Eddie and I talked about it. There had been some trouble at the jail, as I had suspected, but not enough to keep me out. Eddie expected more and shook his head with me over the futility of the whole situation. We talked a long while about the general problem, and some about his case. The newspapers had picked up Mr. Justice Marshall's crack about Eddie and he was upset about it, but I told him the argument had gone well otherwise and I thought the Justice would vote for us anyhow and that we'd win. But the times were far from propitious for trying to get a thrice-convicted shotgun murderer turned loose in the streets on a technicality. Even liberals were beginning to wonder whether "the Warren Court" hadn't gone too far in the direction of putting individual rights of criminals above society's need to protect itself—as the conservatives had charged right along. And with society seeming to be coming apart at the seams in every direction, it was a lousy time for Eddie's case to be coming up for decision, no doubt about that.

Not that Eddie's case had anything to do with all the trouble. It didn't. But all the trouble was part of the atmosphere in which Eddie's case would be decided, and sometimes atmosphere is more important than the merits of a case in determining its outcome. That's why timing is so crucial to litigation, and why landmark advances in human liberty rarely come in times of public crisis.

Of course, Eddie's case wasn't going to be any landmark one way or the other. It didn't involve any sweeping change that was going to have a tremendous effect on other prisoners and on law enforcement in general. If we won, Eddie was going to get out of jail—along with Orson White—and in the future, prosecutors in a few cases wouldn't be able to read old testimony—that's all.

We won, all right, with a vote to spare—6 to 3, with Black, White, and Harlan dissenting. Harlan was a surprise because he'd written the opinion I'd relied on in arguing the case, but it didn't matter since we didn't need his vote anyway. And Justice Marshall, despite the crack from the bench, came through, and nobody gave a damn about the riots and all that, though it was June 10, 1968, and the town was still pretty uneasy.

XVII

To Be a Man

(*Eddie*)

After about three months, the case was reversed by the U.S. Supreme Court and a new trial ordered. Al was right; the Supreme Court agreed that the District Court and the Appeals Court were both in error for permitting the use of testimony from a former trial when the witness was available but chose to remain silent. The "fruit of the poison tree" argument had done it.

It was again a time of happiness. There can be nothing but pure joy when a life sentence is taken away. I had a feeling of being clean, like stepping from a pool of sparkling clear water and having it trickle from my body, like having a tremendous weight lifted from my brow—words, words—how can I express the feeling? Is there another feeling to compare with it? There is but one, to be born *again,* to breathe when you were sure that there was not another breath left. I guess it's the same feeling of relief as when the hangman removes the noose, if only for a second; it's off and there's hope—you awaken and find that really it was not you who died, and you silently thank God even when you've convinced yourself that you don't believe in that shit, and you remember . . . you remember the last trial, the injustice, the agony, the defeat, the tricks, the prejudice . . . and you convince yourself that it won't happen again. It can't! You smile, you smile at Al Prather. There's not much to say to Al Prather—he gave you your life. You smile . . . it feels good, it's warm and strong . . . it comes from your heart. The smile is for Al because that's the only thing you have to give him in return.

The government refused to let go even after the Supreme Court reversal. They were very serious about taking the case to trial again. We were all convinced that they were insane to think that they could get another conviction.

My activities at the jail were even more intense than before. My jail experiences were proving invaluable to me. I knew the jail and the effect of being there as well as any penologist in the country, probably even better. I had one other thing—a burning desire to do something about it! Thinking through an idea for a rehabilitation program occupied a lot of my time. I knew from my own experiences the bitterness that a man feels after being sentenced to a prison term, and I also knew from my experiences what I would have done if given a real chance, not just being put on probation but given a chance to earn a decent living, be respected, loved, trusted, and made to feel a part of something important and meaningful. I wanted to be a man, I wanted the same opportunity that all other Americans have. These were my rights and I, like every prisoner in every jail or prison, wanted to exercise them. If given a choice between going to jail or taking part in a program to provide training, education, self-respect, dignity, and at the same time, remain free in the community, it would take about two seconds to make a decision on which one to take.

I played around with an idea for a preventive rehabilitation program. The concepts were there, and while it was still very much in the think stage, it was a lot better than anything else I had seen. I knew why most of the prison programs failed. I don't think anyone really expects them not to. You can't expect a prisoner to feel like anything other than a prisoner when he's locked up, removed from society, without love, compassion, people who care—when he's outcast and persecuted, and knows that he won't be accepted after it's over. These ingredients do not make for an environment conducive to rehabilitation, only more hostility, degradation, rebellion, and crime.

XVIII

"Hot Dog" Young

(AI)

I went to see Eddie and he was the happiest guy in the D.C. Jail. He was really bubbling over. I told him I'd file a motion for immediate transmittal of the Supreme Court's mandate to the lower court to speed his release, and we talked about what he was going to do when he got out.

He wanted to work in the area of juvenile rehabilitation and had a lot of ideas he wanted to get going. And he was grateful, thanking me for sticking with him so long, believing in him, winning for him.

I told him his release was going to put a lot of responsibility on him. The *Evening Star* had already written an editorial against the court's decision and called Eddie's prospective release a "chilling prospect" for the community.

Eddie understood what I was talking about better than I did. He said he knew he'd be carrying a lot of guys' hopes with him out onto the street and he'd never let them down the way another fellow had recently. Seems a model prisoner, a bright young man with the best of prospects, and seemingly rehabilitated, had been released on parole and had almost immediately been thrown back in for assaulting his wife. The hopes of all those still in jail were shattered; they could hardly expect any favors by way of parole or work release or anything leading to freedom. Eddie asked: "When they give a guy a break and he messes up like that, what can the rest of us expect? Why should they trust any of us? It's bad."

So Eddie knew a lot of people were going to be watching him when he got out: a lot of them who didn't know him, with suspicion and fear—a lot of them who did know him, with hope and faith and pride. And I for one had not the slightest doubt but that Eddie would make it on the outside and that he belonged there and would never let anybody down. More than that, he would do a tremendous job in the ghetto steering kids in the right direction. He talked about it:

"You know, Al, in the neighborhood where I was brought up, the hero of the block—the successful man, the one who drove a big black Cadillac—was the gambler. The images of success were the guys with a good hustle who had fancy clothes and plenty of money, while the honest people went around broke in old clothes. How do you expect a kid to grow up in a neighborhood like that and stay out of trouble? He's bound to get in trouble—a little trouble to begin with, maybe, then bigger trouble, then right down here in jail with a long prison term. And when he gets down here, he's exposed to the worst influence in the world, thrown in with all the hoods and hard-case crooks, and by the time he gets out he's learned a lot of the wrong things and he's almost bound to be sent back. Not all of them. A lot of kids can be helped. A lot of them can be kept out of here in the first place if you can get hold of them at the right time in the right way. But you have to give them the right image of success. You have to show them that they can make it honestly if they try. You've got to show them a way to have pride—somebody to look up to and imitate besides hoods and crooks and gamblers.''

I knew Eddie could be such a guy. A dozen white liberals could go down to the ghetto and make speeches to the kids on "honesty is the best policy" and who'd listen? If Eddie said so, a *lot* of people would listen. I went away feeling Eddie was going to do a lot of good when he got out.

If he got out, I should have been thinking. I went to see the U.S. Attorney to get him to help expedite Eddie's release. He wasn't so sure. He wasn't personally familiar with the case, and the fellow who had tried it last had left to go into private law practice, but new assistants were studying the record to see what they had and determine whether they should dismiss the indictment or try Eddie again.

It was, I suppose, the inevitable reaction of a man in his position. He couldn't just take my say-so that the indictment should be dismissed, and he had a million other problems and not enough help and it was going to take a little time for him to find out what he needed and reach a conclusion about Eddie. The delay was maddening, but nothing to worry about.

But as time went on, the newspaper reported things that made me worry—a little bit at first, then more. It was a bad summer. There was sporadic rioting. There was criticism of the lack of law and order as the Republicans warmed up for the convention of 1968. President Johnson wasn't going to run, the Senate rejected Abe Fortas as Chief Justice, Robert F. Kennedy was shot—the whole atmosphere of Washington was despairing. One small item of purely local interest caught my eye. The U.S. Attorney I had talked to about Eddie was one of the people President Johnson was trying to appoint as a judge in the waning days of an already dead administration. He'd have to go before a conservative committee of the Senate that would just love to jump on dismissal of an indictment against a three-time convicted shotgun murderer. Poor Eddie's chances didn't look so good.

They turned out to be lousy. The government decided to try him again. I couldn't believe it. They had absolutely *no* evidence this time. There was *no* way he could be convicted. *No way!*

I talked to George Thomas and to the young Assistant U.S. Attorney who'd been assigned to handle the case. We chatted over coffee in the cafeteria in the basement of the U.S. Courthouse, the scene of many such conversations. The Assistant U.S. Attorney had studied the record of the case and agreed with us. He'd recommended dismissal of the indictment, and the matter had been referred to the Department of Justice. He'd been overruled, so there was nothing he could do but take the case to trial. But he was planning to take a vacation and would we agree to a brief postponement of the trial?

Hell, no, we wouldn't agree, and we'd fight any effort by the government to hold off the trial. He just smiled and said he thought they'd probably get the delay anyway, and they did. Not just once but twice. So it was September by the time we got Eddie back to the District Court to be freed.

Even then we had to go through the formality of a mock trial. There wasn't any testimony left that could convict Eddie again or even get the case to the jury, and we all knew it. The government would put on its case, George would move to dismiss, and we'd all walk out of the courtroom with Eddie free at last. Couldn't take more than half a day.

Oh yeah? Ever hear of "Hot Dog" Young? We did, just before lunch. He had testified at the first two trials of this case, but not at the last one. They couldn't find him that time, so they had just read his testimony from prior trials. We knew what his testimony had been and it had nothing to do with Eddie, just with Joe Sampson; and it was not all that damaging, as Sampson's presence on the street for the past two years attested.

So I couldn't have cared less when the government called Young to the stand. But then he started saying surprising things. He identified Eddie and said Eddie had been in a restaurant watching Cider Brown count $4,000 on a table, had followed Brown out the door and followed him away in a car minutes before his death. Oh boy! It was all a lie. I turned to Eddie, who was sitting next to me at the table for the defendant and his counsel.

"Eddie, do you know why he's testifying like that?"

A negative shake of the head.

"Does he have something against you, from the jail or someplace?"

Again a negative head shake from Eddie, and a whispered "I don't know why he's saying that."

Well, you can imagine we raised a lot of hell about that. George and I both made every objection we could think of, and George cross-examined the guy all afternoon and proved conclusively that he was either hopelessly confused or a bald-faced liar. We argued till we were blue in the face for dismissal, but we lost. Instead of being a free man, Eddie was now a four-time convicted first-degree murderer.

I wasn't just sick—I was mad. Mad clear through. The government of the United States was putting Eddie away for life on the basis of false testimony, and everybody in that courtroom should have realized it—the judge, the prosecutor, the clerk, the marshals, the court reporter, the jurors, the spectators—and Eddie. Eddie, with his high hopes of helping kids go honest, not twenty steps from freedom—Eddie was being hauled away to jail again by a dishonest government.

I told him not to worry, I'd get it reversed. Eddie smiled wanly, his eyes reflecting the shock and dismay of being right back where we'd started so many years before. He shook my hand firmly and walked toward the door leading to the prisoners' cage behind the courtroom.

Some big deal winning a case in the Supreme Court. That plus fifty cents will get you a cup of coffee at the best restaurant in town. If you can only find a way to get out of jail to go there, that is.

XIX

Something New

(Eddie)

The burden of a life sentence was again placed on me. But I had learned to wear it with dignity.

It had been a mistake for me to think that I would ever get out of prison through the court, but mistakes are worth making if they turn out to be learning experiences. After the fourth trial I was able to convince George Thomas to file a motion for my release on bond pending appeal. The trial court denied the motion almost as a matter of course, and I was returned to jail to finish serving my time.

With some of the other lawyers who were assigned to represent me, I sometimes found it necessary to take matters into my own hands. Al and I had agreed that I would not interfere with his handling of the case, but I was beginning to be less confident that we would ever win this case on its legal merits.

I had tried to be patient, but it just wasn't paying off. The living conditions at the jail for me weren't bad at all; as a matter of fact, I had all the conveniences of home—a fact

which began to frighten me. I was comfortable at the jail—
and that was a sure indication that it was definitely time to
leave. I was becoming institutionalized, much too involved
in the functions of the jail. I had almost forgotten that I was
a prisoner! "Wake up, fool, it's not your job to run this
fucking jail!" For two whole days I walked around the jail
seemingly in a daze, not responding to people or things,
looking at the stone walls, the guards, the bars, realizing
that I was in a jail and the only person who was going to
get me out was *me!* I thought more about the motion for
release on bond that had already been denied; the government opposition was kind of weak, based mostly on the
seriousness of the charge, the fact that I had been convicted
on three previous occasions, and the fact that I was sentenced to life imprisonment and had nothing to lose by
running away.

I began to put together another motion for release on
bond pending appeal, but this time it would be together!
I talked to Al about the motion and he told me to go ahead.
The Bail Bond Reform Act of 1966 was established to in-
sure more uniform bail practices. The right to bail was
clearly established by the U.S. Constitution, but the actual
practice allowed only the rich to benefit from it. Bondsmen
across the country were taking out only the people considered low risk, which usually meant middle-class white-collar criminals. The poor people were not let out on bail
because they couldn't afford to pay the bond premiums or
because the bond was too low for the bondsman to make
a profit. The Bail Bond Reform Act allowed people the
right to bail on their personal recognizance regardless of
charge or sentence. The only stipulation was to make a
showing to the court that you would return when called on,
not be a danger to the community, have a place to live, have
a means of earning a livelihood—and that you would not
flee the jurisdiction. If the court needed a showing, a showing they would get. "All right society, I've played it your
way; now let's try it my way."

I was very busy talking to some of the officers about writing letters to support my motion for release on bond. Most of them were willing to help, but only a few of them would actually take the time to sit down and write the letters. That was easy—I drafted them myself, for their signature. I studied the Bail Bond Act very carefully and made sure that the language of the letters answered every point. I was going to win this one!

Working on the motion for release was very good for me spiritually and emotionally. The chances were good; it was no longer a matter of law but more of an appeal to the conscience of man. Instead of being demoralized and accepting the sympathy of well-wishers, I had a renewed spirit and determination to be free.

In the meantime Maurice Lewis and I were putting together a recognition banquet for the inmates. It was to be the first social event ever held at the jail. A number of people from the Outside were invited—judges, civic groups, church and Redskin members. The event was to honor the inmates who had been outstanding in sports events or had made some other type of significant achievement while in the jail. Judge John P. Fauntleroy of the Juvenile Court was among the judges who attended and I sat next to him at dinner. We talked about the banquet and the other types of programs I was working with at the jail. I was very interested in talking to some of the young kids who were before his court and he promised to see what he could work out. We ended up talking about my case and the fact that I was preparing a motion for release on appeal bond. He didn't believe the incredible history of my case, nor did he agree with some of the decisions made in the case by some of the judges. I promised to write him a letter explaining more of my ideas for preventing juvenile delinquency.

Write him a letter I did! Judge Fauntleroy made arrangements for me to visit him on a number of occasions in his chambers. I had never met a judge before and wasn't aware that there was more to them than black robes and dumb decisions. Judge Fauntleroy was a good human being to begin with, and with that quality as a basis, you can't go very wrong. He agreed to write a letter in support of my motion for release on bond. He also offered job assistance if I were released! My letter campaign was going very well. I could see the end of the road.

XX

*Help Along
the Way*

(Al)

Eddie and I were conversing at our usual spot, across the shiny surface of a table in the rotunda of the D.C. Jail. Eddie had a manila file folder and was pulling out papers for me to read. They were written statements supporting his application for release on bail—some typewritten, more handwritten, all with one theme: Eddie was thoroughly rehabilitated and trustworthy and could be of service to the community on the outside. They told of his good works in the jail, and they were signed by people who ought to know—jail officials.

Of course there wasn't any application for Eddie's release on bail; that's what I was there to talk to him about. Eddie wanted me to get him out on bail.

He had developed a kind of one-track mind on that score. Congress had passed the Bail Reform Act a long time before, in 1966, and ever since then Eddie'd had the notion he ought to be able to get out of jail under it. All kinds of guys were, either on complete bail or on "work-release" programs that let them out to work during the day though they had to return to jail for the night.

I say all kinds of guys were getting out, and they were, but not guys convicted of all kinds of crimes. Nobody serving a life sentence for first-degree murder had gotten out that way, and that was Eddie's rap. So up until now I'd discouraged Eddie from even trying. I didn't mind working for free on anything that might make sense or have one chance in a thousand of being successful, but I wasn't going to waste my time on projects that made no sense at all. So I'd always refused to help Eddie seek release on bail when he'd brought it up in the past.

This time it was different, though. I'd started an appeal that *anyone* would have to agree was going to be a winner. You just don't convict a man by knowing use of perjured testimony, so Eddie was going to get out in a few months at most anyway. And he had one hell of a great record in prison. He'd earned his high school equivalency diploma, he'd been active in constructive projects, he'd held positions of administrative responsibility in the jail, he was trusted and liked by prison officials, he'd even *been* loose on the outside once with their permission, to go to the ball game. So he'd demonstrated that he could pass up a chance to run away even if he *was* serving a life sentence, and that ought to help impress a court passing on a bail motion.

Anyway, this time I thought Eddie had a chance, so I was going along with his program for getting out of jail and he was showing me the supporting statements he was collecting. He wanted me to put them in proper legal language and have them typed up pretty and tell him what they should be like for future guidance in getting more.

That I wasn't about to do. The statements he already had were beautiful. Simple, straightforward, obviously from the heart, honest, and moving. Correct all the grammar and spelling, type it all smoothly, give it a "professional" touch and lawyer's language—and you'd ruin the whole damn thing. These statements, just as they'd come from the pens and pencils of the people who knew Eddie in jail, had overwhelming sincerity, and you couldn't *help* but be moved as you read through them.

Eddie was telling me of the other people inside jail and out who wanted to help and would submit supporting statements. One name startled me—Judge Fauntleroy of the Juvenile Court.

I went away thinking Eddie was going to have a great petition for release on bond. It would be very plain and simple. I wouldn't try to argue his case in the petition, just put in the bare facts and let Eddie's supporters do the convincing in those eloquent supporting letters.

I called Judge Fauntleroy's chambers. Yes, he knew Eddie wanted his support, and he would give it. More than that, the judge was also chairman of the organization administering the local poverty funds from the federal government and he would assist Eddie in getting a job in their youth program, where Eddie's talents and energy could be put to good use and he could earn his living. The judge had faith in Eddie Harrison.

When I hung up I just sat there thinking what a great guy this judge was. He was really laying it on the line for Eddie. Maybe you don't know what it means to a lawyer to become a judge—how important it is to him. Especially, maybe, a black lawyer. And this particular judgeship wasn't any lifetime appointment, either, but would come up for reappointment in a few years. And signing petitions for prisoners isn't exactly in the normal course of business for a judge; I'd never heard of it before and I don't think the judge had either. But he didn't hesitate. He laid it on the line for someone he believed in. He's some kind of man in my book.

I took care of the few formalities needed, collected the remaining statements, and filed the petition very hopefully. It looked to me like Eddie was going to get himself out of

jail if anyone in his position could. But that was a big "if."
Nobody had ever been turned loose yet on "personal
bond" when he was serving a life sentence for first-degree
murder, and maybe none ever would be. It sounds a little
risky. It is a little risky. You know what "personal bond"
is? It's just a promise you'll turn yourself in and go back
to jail if you lose your appeal. Turn yourself in to serve a
life sentence? Would *you?* Would Eddie? Should a court
take that chance? Would it?

XXI

Strange Freedom

(*Eddie*)

The motion for release on bail was ready and filed with the Court of Appeals on September 22, 1968. It would take a while to hear back from the court, but I found plenty to occupy my time. Jail is a lonely place, but it doesn't have to be, especially if you know the system well enough to make it work in your favor. I was seeing my girl friend again but unable to touch her for more than a fleeting second. I couldn't satisfy her sexual needs any more than she could mine, nor could I deny them. The nights are lonely, horribly lonely, the sheets are cold to the touch, and empty—no warmth to share, no thigh or breast for comfort, no face to kiss, only bitter frustration, unfullfilled desire, and memories.

Caroline was a member of the clerical staff of the Work-Release unit. She had recently come to work at the jail. Tall and brown, long black hair, full-breasted and graceful. Keen facial features, deep dark eyes, beautiful white teeth. She had a natural quality of sensuality, earthiness, and womanliness that eminated from her like the sweet smell of a field of honeysuckle. I was drawn to her, even against my will. I watched her body move across the courtyard and fantasized that each step was actually a thrust at my body. Her hips jutted out almost as if they were responding to my fantasy. If the courtyard were longer I probably would have been able to reach a most glorious climax just watching her walk. My body was starved for sex and ached for relief. Daily I watched her cross the courtyard; she occupied my thoughts day and night.

She soon became aware that I was watching her. She would come to the officers' lounge every day on her lunch hour and watch TV. Whenever she was there I would make constant trips through the lounge to the officers' locker room just to get another glimpse of her. I was jealous whenever one of the officers would talk to her. She talked easily and responded quickly.

Without speaking to her, I loved her. Even before I knew her name I loved her. Every man dreams about a woman who is everything he cannot find in reality—and women were not a part of my reality. Caroline appeared to be all that I had dreamed of and more. I wanted to touch her, to crush her to me, to pour my heart out to her. She smiled at me occasionally and with a quick glance over her shoulder would catch me watching her as she returned across the courtyard. We began to speak to each other. First there were just brief "Hi's" in passing, then gradually a few more words. One particularly painful night I was unable to sleep for thinking about her, and I decided to write her a letter. After about two hours of writing I was able to rest. It had been said. I was surprised as hell the next day. As she was sitting in the lounge, I touched her on the shoulder and handed her the letter: "Here, this is for you." As I started to leave, she said, "Wait a minute, I have something for you!" I quickly took the envelope she handed me and placed it in my pocket. She got up and walked to the employees' bathroom without looking at me. I returned to my office and went into the printing shop and locked the door. Reds was running the press as I came in. I took the letter from my pocket.

"I thought you were going to give her the letter, man."

"I did. This is from her!"

Her letter was basically the same as mine. She felt attracted to me; the height of her day was to come to the officers' lounge to watch me! She had sleepless nights thinking of me, she wanted my body!

"Hey, Reds, give me a drink, man!" Reds got the bottle marked "Blanket Wash Solution," which was actually filled with 100 proof vodka. We both got high, but I don't think my high was from the vodka. Shortly Caroline and I had a full-fledged love affair going. We had sex at least three times a week in the employees' bathroom and sometimes in the Superintendent's office. All of the inmates knew about the affair and soon the officers learned about it. No one ever said anything, because of the scandal it would create. Our affair lasted about six months, six beautiful quick months.

It ended at five thirty one Tuesday morning. I was asleep when Officer Tremble came to my cell.

"Hey Eddie, wake up, you are being transferred to Lorton!"

I was up quickly. "What the hell are you talking about?"

"You are on the Lorton list, man, that's all I know!"

I made a quick call to the captain's office when I got downstairs. I could tell that the order had come from his office and that I wouldn't be able to prevent the transfer.

After I was transferred, Caroline quit her job and I put her on my visiting list at Lorton. I was just in time for the annual family day affair. Once a year Lorton permits visitors to come into the institution and spend a day with the inmates. Caroline came to visit me and we spent the day walking around the yard. There were all kinds of events and games. It was almost like a family picnic. Caroline and I had pictures taken lying on the grass. I sent one to New York Reds with the caption, "Nothing changed."

Because of my work at the jail and my knowing a lot of the people in Lorton, I was given my choice of jobs. I chose to work in the prison chapel. It was one of the easy jobs that would keep me away from the institution as much as possible.

It didn't take long to find out what was happening at Lorton. I soon knew what made the institution live; I could feel its pulse and anticipate its moods. There was a lot of drug traffic in Lorton and because of it a lot of corruption. There was also a lot of fear there; sexual assaults were common and expected. The guards didn't interfere with the inmates very much because the threat of riot was constantly in the air and the guards didn't want any part of it. There was also a great deal of division in the staff—the guards were pitted against each other because of rank, seniority, and color. Lorton had always been a black institution staffed with white red-necked guards, most of whom were illiterate Virginia farmers, and with old black Uncle Toms who had been afraid to speak out about the racism in promotional practices. Now there were more younger militant blacks working at Lorton in all positions from Superintendent down to line staff. The whites were dissatisfied and openly voiced the opinion that those "niggers" got promoted just because they were black. There was also the possibility that racial fights among the staff would automatically spread to the inmate population.

In spite of the conflicts, a number of indigenous inmate groups began to grow in Lorton. There were a lot of inmates there who should have been released years ago but were kept there because of legal technicalities, inadequate parole procedure, or just stupidity and ignorance on the part of our criminal justice system—lives wasting away simply because the system doesn't work. Inmates banded together to stop the sexual assaults, control the drug traffic, develop inmate advisory boards and self-help groups. Because of the almost total lack of realistic treatment offered by the institution, the inmates developed their own therapy, counseling, and assistance programs. I worked with the inmate advisory council and started some small musical groups. Most of the inmates wanted to participate in something and the inmate-conceived groups only scratched the surface.

In spite of the administrative problem at Lorton, it is considered one of the most progressive correctional institutions in the country. Even being considered among the best doesn't mean that it is a viable effective correctional institution serving a useful purpose. For every inmate that is able to overcome the hardship, frustration, and agony of prison, ten will be totally incapacitated and unable to function in a free society. The hope of rehabilitation does not lie in sending a man or woman to prison as it exists today. Prison is the single factor that is responsible for the rising recidivism and repeated incidence of crime.

About six months after being sent to Lorton I was called back to the District Court. My case was pending before the Appeals Court and I didn't have any idea why I was being called to the District Court. The jail grapevine had the news waiting for me when I got there. The order to bring me to court said for "release on bond"! I couldn't believe it—I refused to believe it until I was actually released! The one thing that I had learned from all the attempts at freedom was never to count on it until you were actually released. There is no greater pain than the disappointment and agony of returning to jail when you thought you'd be turned loose. I was torn between wanting to shout for joy and not wanting to commit my emotions to yet another disappointment.

Everyone I talked to at the jail was wishing me luck, telling me to write to them when I got time, or giving me messages to deliver to their lawyers and families. I still refused to believe that I was going to be free. There had to be some mistake. I knew Al would have come to see me or called if all of this were true. I hadn't heard anything at all from Al. Surely he would have known!

The bus ride to court all but completely wrecked my nerves. I was very silent—hundreds of thoughts raced through my mind. What would I do if this were some kind of mistake and they actually let me go? Should I tell them that they were letting the wrong man free? The first thing I would have to do would be to go to Al's office; he would know what to do. I was afraid, even mildly trembling. Scared as hell is the best way to put it!

The court bullpen seemed colder than usual. I couldn't stop trembling or pacing up and down the floor. Time stood still; minutes seemed like hours; the room got colder and colder.

My name was called and I quickly walked to the front of the cold steel cage.

"I see you finally made it, Eddie." I knew the marshal's face, but none of them had names. "You be a good boy and don't get into any trouble out there!"

"You be a good *boy,* too!" I said.

I was led to one of the courtrooms on the second floor and stood before the judge. He read the order of release from the Court of Appeals.

While listening to him read, I still couldn't believe that it was true. I had conditioned myself so damn well to not reacting that it was very hard to let the truth sink in.

"You will report to the probation office and sign the release agreement; thereafter you are free to go!"

I am free to go . . . still no reaction. I followed the marshal out of the front door of the courtroom and down the hallway to the probation office. The marshal presented my release papers to the clerk. I was told to read the conditions of my release and sign them. The conditions didn't matter. I would be free—that's all that mattered. After signing the papers, I was told to go and see a Mr. John Williams, who would be my probation officer. Waiting for Mr. Williams, I had a chance to read the conditions of my release. The only one that bothered me was having to live with my common-law wife. I would have to talk to Mr. Williams about that one; my relationship with her was all but nonexistent and I didn't think it would work out.

After waiting about fifteen minutes I was called into Mr. Williams' office. We talked for about an hour. He explained that I would have to call him at least once a week and that I would have to get a job immediately. He also told me to call him as soon as I got settled in at home. I told him of the possibility of my not moving in with my common-law wife and he seemed agreeable. Mr Williams gave me a bus token and told me to report the following week. I walked out of the court building and stood in the sunlight. Now I believed it . . . I was free!

I stood in front of the court building for about ten minutes, fighting the urge to run, just take off and run like hell. It was a bright day, fairly warm and clear. Dressed in prison clothes with a bus token in my pocket, I pondered what to do. After eight and a half years in jail, the thought of getting on a bus was out of the question; I had no idea where I would end up and I wasn't going to take a chance of getting lost on a bus. Just standing in the fresh air with the knowledge that I was free was enough for right now. I needed time to think. People looked at me. It was obvious that I was fresh out of jail, but I didn't care; they could look all they wanted to. I was free!

Nothing but good has happened to me since the first day I walked out of that courtroom. Fate, luck, destiny, or whatever seemed to be on my side for a change. I decided to walk to Prather's office and before I had gotten two blocks I heard my name called. "Eddie, what in the hell are you doing out here?"

George Thomas had a complete look of shock on his face. "What are you doing out here?"

"I was released on personal bond an hour ago!"

He grabbed my arm and hugged me "Where are you going?"

"To Al's office."

"Come on, I'll drive you." We walked to where George's car was parked. "Do you have any money?"

"No, all I have is a bus token."

"Here is five dollars—no take twenty, damn it."

We drove to Al's office on L Street and parked. Al was out of his office and I told his receptionist that Eddie Harrison stopped in to see him and that I would be back later that day.

"You're Eddie Harrison?"

"Yes!"

For the second time that day, I saw shock and disbelief on someone's face. "I'll tell him you were by, Mr Harrison."

George offered to give me a ride wherever I wanted to go, but I didn't know where I wanted to go; I didn't want to go anywhere in particular. "I think I'm just going to walk around for a while, George; I'll call you tomorrow and we can sit down and talk."

I walked for hours, just looking at things, stopping on the red and going on the green, dodging people and cars. My thoughts were running wild. I was free—and crazy with happiness. I reflected on the lonely nights, the horrible feeling of not really knowing if I would ever get out of jail, the promises I had made to myself and to God that if I ever got out I would never return. But how many times had I heard others make that same promise? I had always thought anybody who returned to prison was out of his goddamn mind—it wasn't going to happen to me. I felt very small and at a great disadvantage, but I was going to make it or die trying.

I didn't have any ideas of how long I had been walking, but it didn't matter—I had all the time in the world. I stopped at a phone booth and realized that I didn't have a dime. I went into a store and bought a soda to get change. Al still hadn't returned to his office so I walked some more. I wasn't going anywhere and that didn't matter, either. What do you do on the first day of the rest of your life? Enjoy it—the simple joy of walking satisfied me. I had a lot of pieces to put together and I wanted to be alone. I thought about my mother and the joy that she had been cheated out of, and I remembered the promises I had made to her. I had promised a lot of people things and I thought it was about time to start paying off!

I found another phone booth and called Caroline. "Hi, what are you doing?"

"Just ironing some things," she said. "How are you?"

"I'm okay." She thought I was calling from Lorton. I decided to play with her for a while. "Gee, I wish I could see you today—I miss you."

"Yeah, I wish I could see you, too, but we'll have to wait until Sunday."

"What if I insisted on seeing you today?"

"Aw come on, it's not like you were back at the jail, you know."

"I went to court today!"

"Oh yeah—what happened?"

"They turned me loose!"

"What do you mean?"

"They turned me loose, damn it, don't you know what that means?"

"Where are you calling from?"

"Ninth and S."

"Eddie, don't play with me like that. Please don't do that to me."

She was crying—hopeful tears, unbelieving tears, happy tears. . . .

"Eddie, are you out, baby?"
"Yeah, I'm out. I'll be up there in a few minutes."
"Oh, hurry up, please hurry up!"

XXII
Cell Block to Cosmos Club

(Al)

I had been out of my office on business, and when I returned there was a message slip on my desk saying that Eddie Harrison had been in to see me while I was out. I called the receptionist to make sure she hadn't accidentally checked the wrong box on the form; maybe he had just called me on the phone. No, he'd been there, right in the office. After all these years of waiting to walk Eddie out of jail, they'd let him out without telling me and he'd come to see me in my office and I wasn't even there! I called the court to find out what was going on—there had to be an order. Yes, there was an order, and a copy would be mailed to me. Mailed, hell, I sent for it right away. It was true: Eddie was out on personal bond pending appeal of his conviction.

Eddie came in to see me later that afternoon. It was hard to believe I was looking at him in an office, not across a jail table. We went over the terms of the court order specifying the things he was to do and not do as conditions of his remaining free. They weren't onerous at all. He was not to leave the metropolitan area, he was to report regularly to a probation officer, he was to get a job, he was to live with his wife and sons.

That last was kind of funny. Eddie wasn't legally married, just common law, and I'd put that on the application to the court. But the court order considered him married and said he was to live with his wife. Later he married her, but for a while there he was under court order to live with a woman he wasn't legally married to on pain of going to jail. Now there was a gal who had something a lot better than your old marriage certificate.

I saw Eddie many times over the next few days and weeks. Judge Fauntleroy got him a job, and he loved it. He was working in a training program for underprivileged kids who wanted to improve themselves and get ahead—right up Eddie's alley. He was a foreman in the program, directly responsible for a number of trainees, and I know those kids had the most dedicated guy in the world working for them.

He got another job, too, and the way that came about was a caution. I got a telephone call the week after Eddie got out. Herb Hughes was calling because of a newspaper article he'd seen on Eddie's release. Seems he was in the consulting business here in Washington. He had an out-of-town client called Learning Systems, Inc. Learning Systems was in the education business, particularly in the field of training programs for prisoners; they had contracts with state governments and the Department of Justice to design and help implement new types of rehabilitation and educational programs that would really do some good for inmates, not just keep them busy. One of their current big contracts was for the new Kennedy Youth Center being built in Morgantown, West Virginia. A Mr. Jonathan Peck was president of the project and he'd seen a story about Eddie's release and wondered what kind of guy he was, whether he was smart and articulate, whether he might be worth talking to in the light of his rather unique experience.

I gave Mr. Hughes an earful about what a great find Eddie would be for them, and he said he'd have Peck call me if that was okay. In a few minutes Peck called me from Massachusetts and I went through the whole dissertation about Eddie again. He was definitely interested in talking to Eddie and said he'd like to see the two of us for lunch next time he was in Washington, which would be soon.

So one day I was sitting at my desk when the phone rang again and it was Messrs. Peck and Hughes, wondering if Eddie and I could have lunch with them at the Cosmos Club.

Now if you're from Washington you know what the Cosmos Club is. It may or may not be the snootiest private men's club in town, but if anyone is listing the top half dozen, it's *got* to be high on the list. It used to be in Dolly Madison's house down on Lafayette Square across from the White House, but it had moved to a mansion out on Massachusetts Avenue in the heart of embassy row. It has one of the swankiest clubhouses in town and a most elite membership. You can't become a member there just by being rich or prominent; you have to have accomplished something scientific or literary besides, like writing a book. And its membership list—past and present—reads like *Who's Who.* Peck and Hughes were beginning to impress me.

I told them I'd see if Eddie was free for lunch and call them back. I called Eddie and he said sure he was free, and he'd come on over to my office right away. I called Peck and Hughes, and they said fine; they had a car and would pick us up in front of the building where my office was.

Eddie called back. He wondered if he should go home and dress up since he was just dressed for work and looked a little sporty. I knew what that was all about and I laughed. Eddie had always shown up in court in a navy blue suit, white shirt, and dark tie, looking very gentlemanly. One day he came in a checked sport coat with an open-necked yellow shirt; I'd given him hell and he'd never come to court dressed informally again. Good old careful Eddie never forgot anything you told him, so he was checking.

I told him not to worry—we didn't have to face any jury today, and I was sure these guys wouldn't care what he had on and it wouldn't matter if he was a little sporty.

A *little* sporty did I say? You should have seen Eddie when he showed up at my office. He had on the brightest, shiniest chartreuse pants you ever saw, a bright green turtleneck, a double-breasted navy blue blazer, and a jazzy leather trench coat. He looked about as much like the Cosmos Club as a stripper in church! And we'd never even met these guys who were taking us. Can you imagine? I thought it was wonderful!

Well, we went down front to wait for them, and sure enough here came a car poking along with two fellows peering at the sidewalk for somebody they didn't know, and when they saw us they pulled over and introduced themselves, but the expression on their faces was kind of funny as you might expect.

It was even funnier when we got to the club. I know Hughes was afraid they wouldn't let us in—at least he seemed kind of relieved when they did—and the next thing you know we were plopping down around a coffee table in one of the fanciest rooms in town. That second-floor ballroom at the Cosmos Club is really elegant. Genuine Louis XV. It was imported bit by bit from a European palace, I'm told—crystal chandeliers, wall paintings and all—and it is just about as formal and elegant—there's no other word—as anything you can imagine.

So here we were, just about as far from the D.C. Jail as you can get, with Eddie in this wild getup and these two strangers inviting us to order drinks, which we all did except Eddie, who had ginger ale. Then all of a sudden it was quiet and somebody had to say something.

Peck was the one who did it. He started rambling along

about his organization and their program and how he'd wondered after reading about Eddie whether he had a contribution to make to it; but his tone and manner made me feel that he thought he'd made a horrible mistake, that Eddie wasn't going to exactly fit and he was really sort of apologizing in advance for what was going to turn out to be a disaster.

But it didn't turn out that way at all. Eddie started talking and they perked up. He was everything they had been hoping for and more. He was full of words, full of ideas, completely at home in these strange surroundings, and he soon put everybody completely at ease. The conversation went on endlessly through another round of drinks and a big lunch in the dining room, where we were the center of a lot of attention from people who must have thought Eddie was some kind of visiting celebrity. He was, of course, though not quite the type they would have imagined. And by the time lunch was over we were all on a first-name basis, back in Hughes' office signing Eddie to a fifty-dollar-a-day consulting contract, and you'd have thought Eddie had been doing this sort of thing every day for the last ten years. I tell you, he *owned* those guys by the time we walked out, he was that good. I couldn't have been prouder if he'd been my own son. It was fascinating to see what this kid could do when you gave him a chance.

And that was just the beginning. Within a few weeks Eddie called me and said he needed some help. He'd been invited to participate as a panelist at a regional conference of federal and state prison educational officials. He wanted to go, and his expenses would be paid, but the meeting was being held in Fredericksburg, Virginia, and he couldn't leave Washington without a court order and what should he do?

I filed a petition with the court and they let him go. He had a great time and learned a lot—and I expect taught a lot—and then he wanted to go again, this time to Pennsylvania and New York and Boston to work on projects of Learning Systems, Inc. The court let him go, and this kid was really beginning to get around.

But then the axe fell. We lost the appeal. It was impossible, but we did. We had a damned tough court by anybody's standards, presided over by no less than the circuit's then leading conservative judge, the Honorable Warren E. Burger.

Familiar name? That very summer, while we were waiting for the court's decision on Eddie's appeal, President Nixon appointed him to be Chief Justice of the United States Supreme Court, replacing Earl Warren. He was the strict constructionist who was going to bring a little law and order around these parts.

It was on the day of his swearing-in ceremony that I got a call from my old buddy Al Stevas at the clerk's office of the Court of Appeals. Al had been helpful at many turns in Eddie's case. They were getting out all of the cases Judge Burger had sat on that were still pending, and they had a decision in Eddie's case, signed by the judge before he left the court. Eddie had lost, Al said, but there was a footnote at the end of the opinion suggesting a further course of action. It was too bad that Eddie would have to go back to jail for a while, but it should be okay eventually. The court was suggesting executive clemency.

I zipped down to the courthouse to get a copy of the opinion. It said Eddie's conviction would stand because if Young's testimony was true, it was enough to warrant the conviction, and it was up to the jury, not the Court of Appeals, to decide whether the testimony was true. Then there was this footnote. This extraordinary footnote. I read it about six times to make sure I understood it. It went like this:

> From his arrest at the age of 18 in 1960 until last Fall
> when he was released by this court on bail pending ap-

peal—some eight and one-half years—Appellant was continuously in custody. Representations made to this court in connection with that bail application, including those by correction officials, suggest that Appellant has gained the regard of the prison authorities and he may have some unique contribution to offer by reason of his own unusual experience. We are, therefore, in the position of affirming a conviction which, because it carries a mandatory sentence of life imprisonment, is beyond the power of any court to alter; at the same time we are aware of significant indications that some of the rehabilitative purposes of imprisonment may already have been achieved. If we believe, as we must, in these concepts, there is a duty to recognize such manifestations and encourage such progress. This would be no problem if the parole authorities were able to bring their powers to bear on Appellant's case, but the statutory limitations upon eligibility for parole in the case of a life sentence prevent that for several years to come. It may be that consideration will be given outside the judicial process to a modification of Appellant's sentence which would give the parole authorities, in turn, an opportunity to review Appellant's situation; this is the purpose of executive clemency powers.

That was some surprise. Here it was, the day of Burger's swearing in as Chief Justice—he was the tough, strict judge who was supposed to save us all from the crooks—and here he was saying that Eddie Harrison was properly convicted of first-degree murder but shouldn't have to go back to jail!

That man was ten feet tall in my eyes right then, and growing every minute. He was as conservative as I was liberal on the law, and I disagreed with the rest of the opinion, but man, talk about justice and humanity and guts, this guy had depths I'd never realized.

I called Eddie and he came by the office to talk about it. The footnote was great, but it did present this little problem of Eddie's having to go back to jail while a pardon was processed. And of course, there might not ever be any pardon, no matter what the footnote said, because granting pardons is the President's business, not the court's. So it wasn't all roses by any means, because that decision was going to become final in a few days and Eddie was going to have to turn himself in unless I could do something fast to buy him some time—and he wasn't too keen on going back to jail after a year of freedom.

He said he had wondered what was up because he'd been followed for the past few days. It hadn't bothered him. In fact, he said, it was kind of nice knowing the police were looking out for him. But now it was obvious somebody was playing it safe to make sure he didn't try to run off when he got the word. Of course there was no chance of that anyway, but the government couldn't know for sure that Eddie would go back of his own accord if he had to. He looked at me with steady eyes and said quietly and calmly, in a matter-of-fact way, that he would arrange things for his family in case he had to go back, but he sure hoped I could do something.

I could, of course, easily enough. I could file another petition for certiorari in the Supreme Court—I thought the opinion upholding Eddie's conviction was dead wrong. But that would only be buying a few months at most because it wasn't too likely the Supreme Court would grant certiorari in the last case decided by its new Chief Justice—especially not in response to a petition alleging that he had condoned perjury—which they knew damn well was an outrageous charge. But that's what it seemed to me the court had done, and I didn't think their reason for doing it would hold water, so I had no compunction about filing the petition. And that would at least give us time to get to work on the pardon route suggested by the footnote, with Eddie on the outside where he could be some help in the effort.

What could he do? I didn't know, but I'd find out. I got out the law books to see what they said about pardons.

They said you filed an application with a Justice Department official called the "Pardon Attorney," that he sent them on with his recommendation to the Deputy Attorney General, who passed them on with his recommendation to the Attorney General, who passed them on with his recommendations to the President, who decided the matter once and for all. Not a bad chain beginning with just one lower official, then Kleindienst, Mitchell, and Nixon, all people who would be likely to think twice about a recommendation from their new Chief Justice!

I went down to the Pardon Attorney's office to find out how the game was played. He wasn't there, but a kindly lady in his office gave me the necessary forms and said she'd have him call me—that it wouldn't do any good to talk to him until he had the filled-in application and had a chance to check Eddie's prison record, and where was he imprisoned?

She was surprised to find he wasn't in prison, and I gathered that was a bit irregular and was going to cause some problems. Nevertheless, she was very nice and I went on back to the office to study the forms and await my call from the Pardon Attorney.

He called and we discussed the case. It turned out it *was* a little unusual and contrary to the rules and regulations to be processing a pardon application for someone in Eddie's position; he wasn't eligible for pardon at all under the rules, because he hadn't been out of jail for at least three years. There was one other possibility, a commutation of sentence, but he wasn't eligible for that either under the rules, because he wasn't in jail. However, in view of that footnote, we should go ahead and put in an application anyway and just ask for a waiver of the rules; then he would give it consideration and process it on up the chain of command anyway.

I put together the application. There wasn't much to it, really, as far as the form went. The important part was the "endorsements"—letters from others saying why Eddie should go free. Eddie had lots of friends who wanted to help him, and he would get the letters. I told him we wanted quality not quantity and left the job to him, while I went on vacation.

When I got back, Eddie had an imposing array of people supporting him. Judge Fauntleroy again. Plus Peck and Hughes, of course, and his probation officer. Also Sylvia McCollum from the Federal Bureau of Prisons, who had invited him to participate in the conference for correctional officers in Fredericksburg; plus officials of the United Planning Organization, where he worked, and officials of the Department of Defense, where he'd been working with his trainees—and he was expecting some more. He'd been up on the Hill working with some congressional and senatorial people on youth rehabilitation projects and was going to testify at committee hearings and would probably be getting letters from some offices up there. And he did, from Senator Brooke and Senator Tydings and others.

This kid was fast turning into a lobbyist in a big way. And a P.R. man, too. Seems some newspaper and radio people were interested and wanted to help, and some people in the White House itself—and whoa, whoa, I said!

"Look, Eddie, we don't want any publicity and we don't want a lot of politicians sniffing around this thing until we've got the application filed and have talked to the Pardon Attorney," I told him. "For all we know, that might just kill us quicker than anything we could do. Let's just put the application in and I'll go down and talk to him and see what he advises about all this other stuff."

One good thing about Eddie, he takes advice—unlike most clients, who pay for your advice and then go ahead and do what they damn well please. Not Eddie. He promised to cool it until I'd talked to the Pardon Attorney. How about his going with me and talking to the Pardon Attorney directly? Not yet, not until I'd seen him alone first and explored the territory.

Okay. So I called the Pardon Attorney and made a date to see him the next morning. I bundled up the application and took it down there at the appointed hour. When I walked into the outer office, the lady behind the desk was in tears discussing something over the phone, and another lady was standing at her desk between us with her back to me, and they didn't see me right away. When they did, the nice lady at the desk came out and when she found out who I was she said:

"Oh, Mr. Prather, I don't quite know what to tell you. The Pardon Attorney died unexpectedly last night. He was right here in the office yesterday and. . . ."

Her words trailed off in my mind. What could possibly go wrong next?

I left the application. No doubt somebody would look at it someday, but heaven knew who or when. And we needed fast action to keep Eddie from having to go back to jail.

Situations are never so bad that they can't get worse, and this one did. Before long I got a telephone call from the man who was taking the Pardon Attorney's place until a new one was appointed. He had been an assistant to the Pardon Attorney so he knew the rules. That was a break. At least we wouldn't have to wait forever for a new man to be appointed and find out what his job was all about before he could do anything. Or so I thought. Actually it was a *bad* break. This guy knew the rules too well, and being a professional bureaucrat in a caretaker role for the job, he was going to follow them. And that was bad, because in reviewing Eddie's application he found out that I had filed a petition for certiorari in the Supreme Court following the recent affirmance of Eddie's conviction; so the case was still pending in court, and the rules said the Pardon Attorney wouldn't consider an application as long as court action was still pending.

I tried to talk him out of it but he felt that his hands were tied. He was as nice as pie but he didn't make the rules; he just followed them. So he wasn't going to process Eddie's application while the court petition was still pending.

Well, that's a sensible rule in the usual case, but it sure put us in a bind. The whole idea was to get Eddie's sentence commuted before the Supreme Court acted on his certiorari petition so he wouldn't have to go back to jail if they denied his petition. And it was very likely they would.

How do you get a bureaucrat to do something that's beyond his powers without permission from above? You go over his head—right? And who was next in the chain of command? The top men in the Justice Department and the White House. Any time up to now that would have been fine, because I knew people in positions like that in the Kennedy and Johnson administrations. But this new crowd running the government were all strangers. Republicans. Mostly from New York and California. Whom did I know who might be able to help us?

Robert Simpson. That's not his real name, but he didn't want me to use his real name, so I'll just call him Bob. He was administrative assistant to a Republican senator—a really nice, helpful guy, and thick as fleas with all kinds of people in the new administration. I invited him to lunch to pick his brain a little.

Bob was glad to come. When we lunch, it's almost always at the Metropolitan Club, and that's a wonderful place for people who enjoy the good life, as Bob and I do. We went, as always, to my favorite room in Washington—the second-floor lounge. It's a huge, handsome room, with velvet wall coverings set off by wooden molding on the walls, with soft leather chairs and sofas grouped around coffee tables—a really gentlemanly place to relax with a martini or two before lunch, when you want to get away from the hustle and bustle of offices and restaurants and just talk leisurely. We gassed a while about things in general, and then I told him about my experience at the Pardon Attorney's office.

Bob wasn't surprised, and he had news for me. They didn't grant pardons. Hadn't for a long time. Seems the pardon situation had been scandalous for years and President Johnson had just cut the whole thing off. The problem was that lots of former convicts—not your small time hoods or run-of-the-mill prisoners, but big shots—wanted to get pardons. Not to get out of jail—they'd served their time—but to overcome the stigma and civil disabilities they suffered as convicted felons. They had plenty of money and were willing to spend it on anybody who could help, and they would bribe you at the drop of a hat if you were that sort, and would try to without even knowing how revolting it was to you if you were honest. Bob had rebuffed approaches from many such distasteful people, but some people on the Hill and elsewhere hadn't. When President Johnson found out what was going on, he just cut off the pardons cold to stop the whole mess. The new administration hadn't done anything yet to start them up again, and Bob didn't know what they were going to do about it or when. He wasn't surprised that I was getting a polite runaround at the Pardon Attorney's office, but he would find out what he could for me.

What he found out, eventually, was that the powers that be really didn't want to talk to me about pardons just then. The whole matter was under study, but there was no point in talking cases yet since nobody knew what the policy was going to be. *Something* was going to have to be done, but nobody knew what or, worse, when. So Eddie wasn't going to get any pardon—not soon, anyway—and our last hope of keeping him out of jail was the petition for certiorari in the Supreme Court.

That hope went out the window on December 8, 1969. The petition was denied. We had grounds for asking for rehearing, and I filed a petition seeking it, but with no real hope that it would be granted. Up until now we'd been between a rock and a hard place. Now the squeeze was on and there was no way out. We'd run out of monkey wrenches to throw into the machinery of the law. Whenever the court got around to denying our petition for rehearing —and it wouldn't take long—Eddie would be back in jail, probably for good.

There was only one thing left to do. We went to see the acting Pardon Attorney, a Mr. Lawrence M. Traylor. Three of us went—Eddie, Jonathan Peck, and me.

Mr. Traylor turned out to be a kindly, pleasant man. He was receptive to our story and seemed impressed with Eddie. And he told us one thing we needed to know. He wouldn't be offended in the least by communications in support of Eddie's application—addressed either to him or the Attorney General or the President, from the Hill or elsewhere—or by publicity of any sort. He didn't know whether efforts of this type on Eddie's behalf would help, and he wasn't advocating an avalanche of letters, but—and this was the go-ahead we needed—stirring up interest in Eddie's case wouldn't hurt.

That's what Eddie'd been waiting for—a green light to let his friends help him. And he turned out to have an awful lot of friends. Some of them called me—from Senate and congressional offices, from high posts in local and federal agencies, from the White House itself—some to find out what to do, others to report things they thought I should know.

And there was some great publicity. There's a fellow named William Raspberry who writes a daily column for the Washington *Post*, called "Potomac Watch." He's a youngish fellow, black, can really write, and has a large following. He did a series on Eddie. Not just one column, mind you, but a series of great pieces. And the *Post* ran an editorial supporting Eddie. And Eddie was on several radio programs and some TV shows. Eddie and his application were getting to be awfully well-known in Washington. But that's Eddie's story, not mine.

XXIII

A Beginning

(Eddie)

When I first got out of jail, Judge Fauntleroy referred me to the United Planning Organization for a job. U.P.O. is a Washington anti-poverty agency which offers comprehensive services to the Washington metropolitan area. I had a lot of fears and doubts when I went for my job interview—it was a totally new experience. I remembered all the stories from other inmates who had come out and couldn't find jobs; they always blamed the employer for the fact that they went back and committed other crimes. I didn't have any particular skill to sell or any prior work experience to fall back on. I only had myself to offer and a very deep commitment to help people find a way to help themselves. I had very strong feelings about young kids being victimized by their environment, born in a world without real hope, destined to live in poverty—with prison being the ultimate reality.

U.P.O. was the perfect place for me to start. The agency was staging an all-out war on poverty, implementing social action programs, economic development, job training, community development, health programs, education programs, housing programs. U.P.O. was a people-oriented agency concerned with human development. My years in jail and efforts at developing programs similar to the ones being implemented by U.P.O. were extremely helpful in qualifying me to work with this agency. I was hired as a worksite foreman with a project sponsored by the Department of Defense. U.P.O. was responsible for recruiting and monitoring the training of about 600 young inner-city kids for permanent jobs with the various Department of Defense installations throughout the city. My job was to visit the kids at the training site and supplement the training with group and individual counseling aimed toward preparing them for permanent placement. There were approximately thirty-five kids on my caseload; some needed intensive counseling, while others were able to handle their situations with little assistance.

I visited Judge Fauntleroy occasionally and talked to some of the juveniles who were awaiting court action. It was strange standing in the lock-up talking to the kids. As a juvenile, I had been in the exact same cell, wondering if I were going to be sent away to a training school. Now looking at a kid who obviously was going to walk the same road, I felt a tremendous sense of waste, both of my own youthful years and this young kid's who couldn't do a damn thing about it. The Judge and I spent a lot of time talking about new ways of attacking the problems of juvenile delinquency. The court wasn't able to solve many of the problems. Sending a kid to a training school was like shipping him to a prep school for crime. The answer obviously was to create a system for preventing juvenile delinquency in the first place. Not an easy chore by any means.

It's very frustrating to realize that society programs children to fail and builds yet another system to absorb the failures. Prisons are built to absorb the people that society rejects or people that reject society because they are rejected. Poor people especially suffer the hardships of being outcast, set aside, and programmed to believe that they are inferior; they are made to live under conditions not fit for animals and are not given an opportunity to better themselves or any hope that conditions will be any different for their children. There didn't seem to be any escape. At times I felt very inadequate and unable to do anything about it, while knowing well that something must be done. There are far too many children who have garbage heaps for playgrounds, rusted tin cans for toys—and the American way of life to blame for it. I hadn't realized how much energy and anger I had stored up over the last eight years, but with the restrictions of prison gone I could fight back.

Things happened very fast during the first few weeks of my release. Al told me that he had gotten a call from a consulting firm that was interested in having me do some work for them. He had arranged to meet with them for lunch.

Jonathan Peck and Herbert Hughes took Al and me to the Cosmos Club for lunch. I think I should have been impressed with the Cosmos Club, but it looked to me like a stuffy old building filled with stuffy old men. Jonathan Peck smiled easily and talked about his company. Learning Systems, Inc. was a criminal justice consultant firm; most of its business was with federal and state institutions. I was very quietly drinking a ginger ale and listening to the two men talk. I didn't know exactly what they wanted from me and there was only one way to find out: shut up and listen! As Peck talked, I nodded occasionally or shrugged my shoulders. They wanted to know about me, about prisons and my experience. Peck touched a sore spot when he mentioned that most poeple didn't care enough to do anything about changing the system. At last I took the floor and told him about my ideas for changing the system. I was very excited and could feel anger swelling up in me as I talked about the effect prison had on people and the need for finding an alternative. I told him about the letters I had written to the mayor, congressmen, and judges about the establishment of a community-based rehabilitation center and my commitment to seeing the idea put into action. After our conversation was over, Peck offered to pay me fifty dollars a day to work for Learning Systems, Inc., on a consulting basis, developing ideas for training programs, appraising proposals, and following up on the ideas for a rehabilitation center. More and more things seemed to be going my way.

I was very careful to keep in touch with my probation officer. I was only required to see him once a week, but I visited him sometimes two and three times a week to ask his advice and assistance. He was very helpful and allowed me to do just about anything I wanted to do. I knew that he had to report to the court on my activities and I made sure that his reports would be positive! Judge Fauntleroy was referring kids to me for jobs and counseling. I was able to convince a lot of employers that it is better to give a kid a job than to give him the payroll at gunpoint.

The crime rate in Washington, D.C., was rising to outrageous proportions, and a lot of the crimes were being committed by young kids. The Police Department was asking for money to hire more police and the courts wanted to reorganize and expand. Because of the emphasis on safe streets, a lot of money was being spent on correction, but none of the money was going where it would have any impact on solving the problems. Jonathan Peck arranged through a friend of his at the Bureau of Prisons to have me speak at an annual meeting of the American Correctional Association, to be held in Fredricksburg, Virginia. The conference was very interesting. There were a lot of wardens, guards, judges, prosecutors, legislators, sheriffs, lawyers, and representatives from all aspects of the criminal justice system. I was one of the few ex-inmates at the conference.

I felt greatly outnumbered but certainly not intimidated by the odds. My message was short and to the point. The correctional system was a miserable failure, and unless steps were taken immediately to correct *corrections,* the police, courts, and institutions should be indicted for the perpetration of crimes against the people. If people are going to be held accountable for crimes against society, then it's only just to hold society and our public institutions accountable for crimes against the people!

It would be far better to release every prisoner in the country than to subject prisoners to the dehumanizing conditions of prison. Society would be better protected by never sending a convicted man to prison. Prisons only serve to reinforce negative, hostile, bitter, antisocial attitudes and in fact compound those feelings by the inhumanity and abnormality of prison life. The result is that society has been put in danger by sending men to prison —not protected at all. For every two men sent to prison who are "considered" dangerous, one man comes out who is guaranteed dangerous. After my speech at the conference, I was surprised to find that a great number of people supported my feelings about prisons and the need for alternatives. I had expected to be "jumped on," but I was congratulated for "telling it like it is."

This was the first of many attempts to arouse public support and indignation at the way the correctional system was treating people—or not treating people is a better way to put it. My attempts to focus attention on the issues put me in a very vulnerable position. I was still on bond and could be snuffed out as easily as a candle if I made too much noise. The only way to protect myself was to not be overly critical without having a viable alternative. I had put together a pretty good outline for the rehabilitation center and Jon Peck and I were trying to get support from senators to establish the program. My job at U.P.O. was requiring more and more of my time. It wasn't really a job; I enjoyed working with the kids, most of whom were just a few years younger than I was. There were not many problems with the kids; most of the serious problems were on the part of the supervisors and the establishment. I spent just as much time counseling the supervisors as I did with the kids.

Most of the supervisors were middle-class, slightly over middle-aged whites who could not relate to the trainees in anyway but as supervisors. Most of them saw the trainees as "those underprivileged kids from the ghetto"—who were not as good as regular employees. There were very strong attitudes on the part of the supervisors to deal with. Racism was very apparent in all the departments. There were blacks who had not managed to rise above the level of a clerk in ten years of service and who were afraid to speak out against it. I encouraged my trainees to report any incidents to me where they felt they were unfairly treated. Racism in this country had been overlooked too long and will never stop as long as we pretend it's not there. It was not just a problem for the trainees. I remember my first encounter with racism at the office of the program coordinator for one of the Navy sites.

"Mr. Cruzan, the boy from U.P.O. is here to see you. Shall I have him wait?"

The receptionist was an elderly white woman, around fifty years old, and she probably didn't realize that she had offended me, or care! I passed up the opportunity to say anything to her until I returned:

"Excuse me, miss, you would probably resent me referring to you as the 'fat old white girl wearing the funny looking wig who answers the phone' just as I resent you referring to me as the 'boy from U.P.O.' My name is Eddie Harrison and I am here on official business from the United Planning Organization, do you understand?"

That was probably a little harsh for the old girl, but it served the purpose! From that day on I was called Mr. Harrison, or the counselor from U.P.O.

250

I began to command respect for myself and the trainees. I held periodic meetings with all the supervisors, which more often than not ended up being group counseling sessions.

We were making some progress with some of the senators on the rehabilitation project. Senator Edward Brooke's office was very interested in helping to get a rehabilitation center established. Jon Peck and I had meetings with some people from his staff and were very encouraged at the results.

I had also contacted a number of civic groups and community organizations. There was a great deal of support for the concept of preventative rehabilitation but no one was willing to put up any money. Through Senator Brooke's office, I was able to contact a number of people in H.E.W. and the Department of Labor who could assist me in getting funds for my program. I took advantage of every opportunity to address groups concerned with reforming a system that has proven beyond a doubt that it doesn't work. I was receiving more invitations to speak than I could possibly handle.

I had a real commitment to using the period that I was going to be free in doing something worthwhile. I had no guarantee that I was not going back to prison, and I would receive no prior notice. I had to do it now or forget it! I also took an active part in the community-based correctional programs. In the short period that I had been free, I had managed to meet hundreds of people who were interested in contributing something to the efforts of crime prevention and people who could assist each other in the things they were doing. I was quick to refer them to each other. There is a hell of a lot of fragmentation and autonomy in corrections—no real way to know who's doing what! I had finished a few consulting jobs for Jon, a correctional officers' training program, and a prospectus on the institutional needs as I saw them. I began to work very intensely in one of the halfway houses in Washington, helping residents find jobs and make the transition from jail to community.

As I reported my activities to my probation officer, he often asked me what in the hell I was trying to prove. After thinking about it, I guess I *was* trying to prove something. I didn't feel that I had a lot of time to waste; there was too much that needed to be done. I had had an eight-year vacation and now it was time to work. I was thankful that my energies were directed into positive things. Most prisoners who are released after long periods of confinement have the same energy and sense of urgency to do something, but they also have a lot of bitterness and a sense of being "owed something" by society because of their confinement.

There were not enough hours in the day for me. I couldn't find time to do all the things I wanted to do. I was almost working myself into poor health.

Al Prather and I were seeing or at least talking to each other almost daily. I was keeping him informed of my every move and checking with him for advice whenever I was uncertain about something. Al was very proud of the progress I was making and always encouraged me to follow through on my ideas.

I could actually see where my efforts were having an effect in changing people's attitudes. My daily contacts with my trainees, supervisors, employers, and even co-workers were producing positive and encouraging results. My spirits were very high. I think I had even managed to forget that I was on bond until the day that Al called me at my office to tell me that the Court of Appeals had upheld the decision of the District Court.

"Eddie, I think you'd better come over here right away; the Appeals Court upheld the decision today."

For the first time I couldn't handle receiving this kind of news. A cold chill slowly spread over my body. It took a few minutes to activate my defense mechanism; I clenched my teeth and slowly settled back into my chair. I shared an office with Doug Williams and Carl Bently. They continued to work, unaware of the shock I was going through.

"I'll be over in a few minutes, Al." I walked the few blocks to Al's office trying to figure out what our next move was going to be. The only thing to do at this point was to appeal once again to the Supreme Court. The odds must have been close to 10,000 to 1.

I was really fucked up—all the fears that I might not be able to do things on a long-term basis were now realities. I remembered the day I bought my car shortly after my release. As I signed the contract, I thought how happy I would be if I were free long enough to make the final payment.

Thirty-six months—I'd be glad to pay the car note for three years. Now my wife would have to assume all the debts I had accrued. She just wouldn't be able to do it!

This was the point where many men have succumbed to the temptation of having one final fling at crime before being gobbled up by the system. Jail was a reality; there was no chance of getting free again—why not? Two or three robberies would be enough—why go to Al's office? I knew why he wanted me to come there. I was going to jail for life. Face it, man, life imprisonment is waiting for you when you walk into his office. Don't be a damn fool . . . you're lost. Can't you see that you're as good as dead? What do you have to lose by running? Chances are they will finally catch you, but what the hell, you will have been free a little longer, and the extra time they'll give you won't even matter! Run, fool, run!

Al was pretty shook up when I got to his office. We talked for a while about the decision of the Appeals Court but in upholding the court's decision, there was an unprecedented footnote at the end of the decision which was very encouraging.

From a legal standpoint the opinion of the court was against me, but from a moral standpoint the footnote was very much in my favor! My work since being released had not gone unnoticed. The footnote recommended that a presidential pardon be granted! From a moral standpoint, he was saying that because the total objective of sending a man to prison is to rehabilitate him, and because since my release I had shown that I was rehabilitated, the ends of justice had been served and there was no reason for my return to prison. The only relief, however, was to have the President of the United States intervene and grant a commutation of sentence! The judge was showing us the path to pursue.

Al went to work immediately preparing the petition for writ of certiorari. We also decided to start work on the petition for commutation of sentence. A small note on the bottom of the petition said "Letters of support would be helpful." We decided that for the next few days I would contact the people whom I felt would be willing to help me; I needed all the help I could get and there was no time to lose.

I left Al's office feeling much better. I would be very busy the next few days. The fight wasn't over yet and I'd be damned if I was going to give up without a fight. The order for my return to prison would be held up pending appeal to the Supreme Court so I at least had a few days of freedom left.

The very next day all of the newspapers carried an account of the court's decision. One of the papers had even called my office to get a statement of how I felt about the court's decision. How in the hell did he expect me to feel? I felt like my life was being taken away—and it was!

XXIV

The Door
Opens Wide

(*Eddie*)

One last chance, one final chance at freedom. I had to take my best shot now, no more jivin' around waiting for the court to say the magic word—I had to do it myself again.

I needed support, letters, affidavits, anything! Senator Brooke's office was the first to respond. Ann Cuningham worked on the Senator's staff as a caseworker. Ann is one of the most dedicated persons I have ever known, and unlike anyone I have ever met. She has a quality of humanity and strength of personality so overwhelming it's unbelievable.

Ann listened very intently as I told her of my plight. She was honest in telling me she didn't think we had much chance of getting a pardon from the President, but she was going to give it a try. I left Senator Brooke's office feeling somewhat relieved and very glad to have Ann Cuningham in my corner. I was lucky that she was interested in my case and was going to help me with my campaign for freedom.

She got to work immediately and was able to convince other senators to support my cause. Before long, my case was as political an issue as it was social. Ann and I kept in daily contact planning strategies. She was charged with enthusiasm and never seemed to run out of energy.

Judge Fauntleroy was willing to write another letter for me, and so were my probation officer, co-workers, trainees, all of the groups that I had spoken before. Letters began to pour into Prather's office. If they wanted evidence of my rehabilitation, they damn sure had it. I had worked hard since my release on bond, often without compensation, and now it was paying off. Very few of the people on my training sites had known of my background, but there wasn't one who wasn't cheering for me, not even the "fat old white lady with the funny looking wig." The time was getting short—I could feel it. We had a meeting with the Pardon Attorney, and I could really feel it getting close after our talk with him.

Mary Ann Bailer, a co-worker at U.P.O., suggested that I go and talk to Bill Raspberry, a Washington *Post* staff writer. He usually wrote about national and local issues and was very influential in the black community. Bill spoke with authority and was read by most Washington area residents who wanted to know what was happening. Bill Raspberry's office at the *Post* was hard to find; it really wasn't an office at all, just a cluttered desk pushed off in a corner with an old typewriter next to it. We talked for what seemed like hours—mostly about my case, the years that I had spent in prison, the trials, appeals, and reversals, the time that I had been free on bail, and the fact that I was going to return for the rest of my life. Bill was quick to grasp the implications of my case. He decided to write a series of articles, which were more a commentary on justice in America.

Soon after Bill's first article appeared, I received a number of calls from radio and TV program directors asking me to appear on shows to discuss my case and the application for a commutation of sentence. Several TV representatives came to my office and shot film for news releases. The ball was really rolling; Bill's articles had a tremendous impact on public opinion. I even received calls from well-wishers who just wanted to wish me luck. I saw every day as the last and worked like hell to get everything finished. Ann Cuningham had contacted a lot of her friends, most of whom worked on the Hill in Washington and in some way were involved in national or local politics. We were playing political games—who knows who, or "who owes who."

During the period that the petition for commutation was being prepared, the U.S. Supreme Court denied the petition for certiorari, and I started to make plans for my return to prison.

We had done everything we could. The news of the Supreme Court denial didn't come as a shock, but neither Al nor I was quite prepared for it.

There was only one thing left to do: wait for the Supreme Court to issue the mandate calling for my return to prison. We all waited—Al Prather, Jon Peck, Ann Cuningham, Bill Raspberry, and me. Every day was hell. The commutation papers had been filed, but it was unlikely that they would be acted on before the mandate came down. Business went on as usual for me. I went to work each day and watched the door for a U.S. marshal type to come in and ask for me. I had made it very easy for them. I went home each evening and just sat around waiting for that authoritarian knock on the door. I kept in touch with my probation officer and told him where I could be reached in case of "emergency."

Everybody was watching me to see how I would react when the time came. I could see sorrow and pity in the eyes of my friends. Most of my male friends wanted to do something for me—offered to help in any way they could. A lot of the females offered their bodies in an effort to console me—to show that they knew what I would be faced with in jail. A lot of them offered me a place to stay if I wanted to disappear. There seemed to be more pressure on them than on me. My kids were still too young to understand what was going on, but they knew I would have to leave them for a while.

The days dragged on and on. I realized that I was being followed one day as I went to the airport to pick up Jon. Two guys, obviously marshals, got very excited as I drove toward the airport. I watched them in my rear-view mirror and thought how nice it was to be cared for and looked after.

I tried not to show that I was being affected by the pressure. I appeared very calm on the outside, but I was torn to pieces on the inside! I thought often of my application for the commutation. President Nixon wasn't really known for his concern for black people—and this was the year for law and order. So what chance did a black man four times convicted of murder have of convincing the President of the United States—especially President Nixon—to grant him a presidential commutation of sentence? Pretty god-damn slim, I would say. So what the fuck was I waiting around for? Why not follow Robert Williams, Eldridge Cleaver, and H. Rap Brown?

I felt the same pressures that they had, and had the same natural inclination for self-preservation. My fate was sealed, judgment had been passed. There are few words to express the human emotions of those days, but there is one word to describe why I chose to see it through—defiance!

Nothing had been able to break my spirit. My ego was much too big to let it happen even now. I had invested too much and fought too hard to throw it away. I resisted the temptation to run more out of reflex than anything else. I'll be damned and go to hell before I let this system make me something that I had fought so hard to prove I'm not—a criminal—an animal—less than a man—something that needed to be put in a cage!

Coincidence, design, politics, justice, or just dumb luck, whatever you want to call it, *the order never came down from the Supreme Court to return me to jail!* Somewhere along the line a very heavy sheet of paper was lost. A piece of paper as deadly as a bullet for Eddie Harrison.

As I waited to return to jail, someone or something was turning the wheels of government, pushing aside the red tape, procedures, and bullshit. The commutation was granted on February 28, 1970. Ann Cuningham was the first to know. She called my home but was unable to reach me there. She left a message for me to call her regardless of the time. When I received the message I knew something was up.

"Hi, Ann, this is Eddie!"

"Eddie, your commutation was granted today!"

As simple as that! There were no shouts for joy, just a very powerful sinking sigh of relief. We had won!